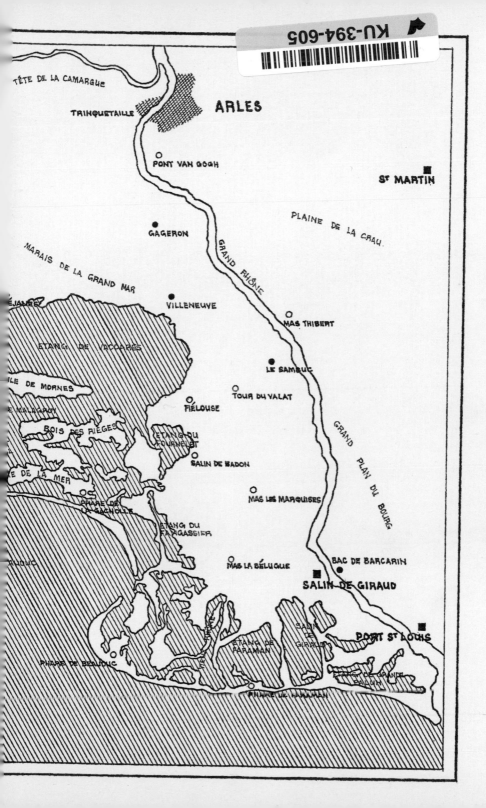

TÊTE DE LA CAMARGUE

TRINQUETAILLE

ARLES

PONT VAN GOGH

S<sup>t</sup> MARTIN

PLAINE DE LA CRAU

GAGERON

MARAIS DE LA GRAND MAR

GRAND RHÔNE

ÉJAMES

ÉTANG DE VACCARES

VILLENEUVE

MAS THIBERT

ÎLE DE MORNES

LE MALAGROY

LE SAMBUC

BOIS DES RIÈGES

TOUR DU VALAT

FIÉLOUSE

A

ÉTANG DU FOURNELET

GRAND PLAN DU BOURG

E DE LA MER

SALIN DE BADON

PHARE DE LA GACHOLLE

MAS LES MARQUISES

ÉTANG DU FANGASSIER

DUC

MAS LA BÉLUGUE

BAC DE BARCARIN

SALIN DE GIRAUD

PHARE DE BEAUDUC

SALIN DE GIRAUD

PORT S<sup>t</sup> LOUIS

ÉTANG DE FARAMAN

ÉTANG DE GRANDE PALUN

PHARE DE FARAMAN

# THE CAMARGUE

# THE CAMARGUE

by

## CAROL DIX

LONDON
VICTOR GOLLANCZ LTD
1975

ISBN 0 575 02034 2

*Printed in Great Britain by*
*The Camelot Press Ltd, Southampton*

*To Marjorie and Bill Dix*

"La Nature, dans ces paysages primitifs et dans ses races pures de bêtes n'est-elle pas, elle aussi, un monument historique admirable et précieux d'autant plus que ce que nous nommons civilisation aura bientôt tout détruit, tout volé?"

MARQUIS DE BARONCELLI-JAVON, 1922

"I do not undervalue the things of a nation's body, I only desire that they shall not make us forget that beside the nation's body there is also the nation's soul."

PRESIDENT THEODORE ROOSEVELT, 1904

"I have never had a chance, nature here being so extraordinarily beautiful. Everywhere and all over the vault of heaven is a marvellous blue, and the sun sheds a radiance of pale sulphur, and it is soft and as lovely as the combination of heavenly blues and yellows in Van der Meer of Delft. I cannot paint it as beautifully as that, but it absorbs me so much that I let myself go, never thinking of a single rule."

VINCENT VAN GOGH, Arles, 1888

# CONTENTS

# LIST OF ILLUSTRATIONS

# ACKNOWLEDGEMENTS

My thanks go to John Walmsley and Dr Luc Hoffmann, of the Tour du Valat, Station Biologique; to Eric Coulet and René Charavin, of the Réserve Zoologique et Botanique de Camargue; to Catherine and Jacques Guillaume, of Port Dromar; to Ludo and Martine Chardenon, the "Plant Magic Man" of Sommières; to Lawrence Durrell; to André Dupuis, of the Cie. Bas-Rhône-Languedoc; to François and Mme Pagès of the Domaine de l'Amérique; to Françoise Puget of the Mas de Grand Gageron; to Hubert Yonnet of the Mas la Bélugue; to Michel Plan of the Mas de Grand Antonelle; to Jacques Blondel of the University of Montpellier; to Pierre Heurteaux of the Centre d'Écologie de Camargue; to Albert Schwerer of the Salins du Midi; to Paul and Mme Chabaud of the Hôtel le Mouton Blanc in Le Sambuc. Also to the Bibliothèque Nationale in Arles; to the French Institute in London and to the British Museum. Mostly, to Pete for the patience and love with which he provided the photographs and bore with my obsessions; to Mary for her help and guiding spirit while the writing was in process; and to Liz for her kind and tactful editorial interest.

I would also like to thank Curtis Brown Ltd, on behalf of the estate of Roy Campbell, for permission to quote the poem, *Horses on the Camargue*.

C. D.

LONDON, 1975.

# AUTHOR'S NOTE

The Camargue proper (or Grande Camargue) is that area, almost an island, bordered neatly by the two branches of the Rhône and by the Mediterranean sea. As a whole, though, the term also includes the Petite Camargue, which westwards supports similar vegetation and way of life; and eastwards includes the Crau which continues the way of life, but alters in habitat. But the Camargue in question now is the triangular delta. Outside its riverain confines, the land is unprotected by Reserve or Regional Park. Because of that, ironically, some parts of the Petite Camargue are less touched by human interference than any other part. But that may not remain so. Already property development has begun to press the old way of life further towards the shore. For that reason I am concentrating on the Grande Camargue.

# PREFACE

I SLEPT OUT on the beach on my first visit to the Camargue; attracted there by who knows what beyond an amalgam of impressions I had received from television and books. The mosquitoes were revengeful, the *mistral* did its best to blow anyone's good intentions off course and the world monetary markets decided to destroy an English traveller's last moments of confidence. Driving into the Camargue I'd said, "This feels like going into another country". Finding the two banks in Les-Saintes-Maries-de-la-Mer to be closed for three days, I discovered just how true that was. The fraternity of people sleeping out on the beach had all used up their meagre resources and somebody had to get to a bank. I had a car, some Americans had bicycles. The nearest town was Arles, twenty-five miles away. We all had empty wine bottles. Pooling our resources we bought one franc's worth of petrol, giving the salesman the biggest anti-English kick he'd had for a long time. We drove to Arles and found money. The sun had come out so we hurried back to the Camargue for a few more days.

Entering the village of Les-Saintes again that day, we wondered what all the crowds were doing in the streets. Everyone was rushing this way and that, people were dressed up in riding clothes and a lot of men had gaucho-style hats on. Half an hour later, the streets were quickly cleared for a herd of smallish bulls to hurl themselves down the main road, chased by smaller boys and directed round into the arena. That was my first sight of an *abrivado*. "Carmen" was blaring out over loudspeakers and everyone seemed to be piling into the arena.

So we joined in. The spectacle was free that day as it was the "day of the horse". I knew nothing then about the Camargue's traditions, its indigenous horses, bulls, *course libre* and skilful horse riders, nothing about Provençal separatism, the nine-teenth-century renaissance in Provençal literature and the man who spurred the Camarguais into self-love, the Marquis Folco de Baroncelli-Javon, and little enough about its importance as a nature reserve and the problems besetting the whole area. All that was yet to be learned.

That day in the arena was enormously stimulating—so much enjoyment, so much colour and life, and a completely different atmosphere from the one I expected at a bull-fight. But then this was not a *mis-à-mort*. It was a purely Camarguais game of playing with the bull, daring it to come and hit you and loving it all the more if it did. The games in the arena were followed by a meal for all the townsfolk, under the trees, with roasting ox, freely flowing wine and dancing to toreador music. Their generosity even extended to the people who sleep on beaches and cannot afford petrol.

Later I visited the Camargue in a different guise: as a journal-ist writing a report about the gypsy festival of Les-Saintes-Maries-de-la-Mer. It is held every May and gypsies from all over the world pour into the little town to pay homage to their patron saint and are somehow, if only just, tolerated by the town's officials. There is something about the gypsies that is not so far removed from the spirit guiding the Camarguais. They share a passion for the idea of a free soul, even if we have come to question the meaning of that in today's more cynical world. That time, I also began to feel more involved in the way of life there. My ears were opened to complaints and I noticed news-paper stories about pollution and fears of the Camargue being swamped by rampant industrial growth and real-estate frenzy. So the questions came to mind. Could this quasi-island, so different from anywhere else in France I knew, really survive or hope to? Is it not really rather naïve to pretend to a way of life of some hundred years ago in the super-civilised France of today?

The Camargue is, as most people know, an area of marshes and salty pools, home to wild, white horses, to black bulls and to an exotic display of birds, including the rare and beautiful Flamingoes. As such, it has become an important area to people as well, not only physically, but also psychologically, as a fantasy land where minds can stretch and relax; somewhere that offers expanses of uncultivated territory, where herds of beautiful horses stampede into a sunset, their manes flowing free in the sun and wind  But while the Camargue could not help becoming popular as a holiday setting, the fantasy has misled some people and the fact is that many tourists go away disappointed. Some leave complaining that there is nothing of any interest there. There are no wild white horses, just tame ones corralled ready for rides; the land is covered in tall reeds and public entry is restricted. They find the whole place a bit creepy and depressing—are not sure why it was so strongly recommended.

Sadly, they have not been able to see beneath the superficial impressions and discover the hidden Camargue; for its wildness is still there, though now carefully guarded and protected by the inhabitants; and the way of life, often compared to that of America's Wild West, continues today, but it is kept just out of the tourist's eye. The Camarguais have had to close their doors to any would-be voyeurs. If you want to know what life is like for the Camarguais, then that takes more time and a little more understanding of what made the area the way it is: which, I hope, is what I can offer in this book.

I have also tried to write something more than a history or a straight descriptive work of the area; to show it, in a contemporary light, beset by modern pressures. The Camargue demonstrates well the plight of many interesting and unique areas, whose very individuality makes them much more vulnerable to change. The delta of the Rhône covers an area of only about three hundred square miles, and it stands like a buffer zone of peace and sanity between two high-speed growth spots on the French landscape. To the east is Fos sur Mer, fast becoming the second largest port in Europe and a huge centre for heavy industries. To the west are the buildings of six new holiday resorts, on a super-2001 scale. So, the tiny triangular delta is obviously vulnerable to pollution pressures, to land-grab threats and to the sheer weight of over-population. Its survival will be in question over the next few years.

The southern French, particularly from Provence, are unashamedly romantic about the Camargue and the writers from the area have made the delta a symbol of resistance to change. Half a century ago, a writer who lived in the Camargue, and who has since become accepted as part of French literary history, wrote a fantasy story called *La Bête du Vaccarès*. Joseph D'Arbaud wrote his fable around one of the most mystical areas of the Camargue, the large lake at its centre called the Étang de Vaccarès. There, the story goes, a sixteenth-century peasant found the tracks of an unknown animal. What he eventually met was a terrifying beast with a human face. The beast explained that he was a survivor of a primitive species who, in escaping mankind, had been chased towards the coast into this wild and primitive area, where it hoped to avoid further cruel pressures from man. The beast personifies the Camargue itself—or any other part of the natural world threatened by encroaching civilisation. In this case, primitive beast is being hounded out by man's need for more land and food, and also by newly evolving animal species. The beast himself says, however, "It is a universal law that everything must pass and be transformed, and that yesterday gives way to tomorrow." But he says it with utmost regret and sadness.

Sometimes, the Carmarguais echo D'Arbaud; as one old local said to me, "We have to forget our yesterdays and learn to live for tomorrow." Others are more pessimistic and fearful. With Fos already two years into production, a local hotelier's wife said, "Oh! I don't give the Camargue more than two years. I'm pessimistic by nature but I can't see how the birds and the vegetation can survive with the pollution that will come from Fos, and from the number of tourists who flock here every summer. I came here seventeen years ago to live, and then there were no tourists and no hotels. Mind you, the people with money obviously think that the Camargue will survive as they're still pouring in to buy up new hotels. Maybe it will survive, but it could be as a sort of Indian Reserve where the people act out being Camarguais for tourists, to keep the economy running."

The Camargue remains, though, many things to many people. To the ornithologist it is one of the most valuable wetland zones in Europe, attracting a wide range of birds and many thousands of ducks in winter. To the farmer it is a livelihood from wheat, rice, vines, fruit or tomatoes; to the hunter it is heaven; to the salt manufacturer it is the natural source of mile upon mile of salt pans; to the rancher it is the habitat of the local black bulls for the Provençal *course libre*, and the sturdy white horses; and to all the residents, it is an island which retains a unique way of life, far removed from twentieth-century clamour.

Some things have happened to protect and conserve the way of life on the delta. Of the total area of the Camargue, nearly a third is protected land belonging either to the state Réserve Zoologique et Botanique de Camargue, to the privately owned ornithological station of the Tour du Valat, or to the local community Réserve des Impériaux. The land belonging to the state Réserve takes up the central part of the delta including the Étang de Vaccarès and the mysterious ancient forest known as the Bois des Rièges. The Camargue has also been designated a Regional Park (Parc Naturel Régional de Camargue), a body set up to organise the disparate interests of the area and concerning itself with the growth of towns and villages, the use of agricultural land, the amount of freedom to be given to tourists and the protection of the people's way of life. It is a body without the backing of law, resting almost solely on good will. Will it be enough to ensure that the Camargue we know today will survive, or at least not suffer too many changes?

In the grey wastes of dread,
The haunt of shattered skulls where nothing moves
But in a shroud of silence like the dead,
I heard a sudden harmony of hooves,
And, turning, saw afar
A hundred snowy horses unconfined,
The silver runaways of Neptune's car
Racing, spray-curled, like the waves before the wind.
Sons of the Mistral, fleet
As him whose strong gusts they love to flee,
Who shod the flying thunders on their feet
And plumed them with the snortings of the sea;
Theirs is no earthly breed
Who only haunt the verges of the earth
And only on the sea's salt herbage feed—
Surely the great white breakers gave them birth.
For when for years a slave,
A horse of the Camargue, in alien lands,
Should catch some far-off fragrance of the wave
Carried far inland from his native sands,
Many have told the tale
Of how in fury, foaming at the rein,
He hurls his rider; and with lifted tail,
With coal-red eyes and cataracting mane,
Heading his course for home,
Though sixty foreign leagues before his sweep,
Will never rest until he breathes the foam
And hears the native thunder of the deep.
But when the great gusts rise
And lash their anger on these arid coasts,
When the scared gulls career with mournful cries
And whirl across the wastes like driven ghosts:
When hail and fire converge,
The only souls to which they strike no pain
Are the white-crested fillies of the surge
And the white horses of the windy plain.
Then in their strength and pride

The stallions of the wilderness rejoice;
They feel their Master's trident in their side,
And high and shrill they answer to his voice
With white tails smoking free,
Long streaming manes, and arching necks, they show
Their kinship to their sisters of the sea—
And forward hurl their thunderbolts of snow.
Still out of hardship bred,
Spirits of power and beauty and delight
Have ever on such frugal pastures fed
And loved to course with tempests through the night.

*Horses on the Camargue* by Roy Campbell.
From *Collected Poems*, 1949, Faber & Faber Ltd

# PART I

# CAMARGUE PAST

*Chapter 1*

# THE GREY WASTES OF DREAD

---

ARLES, THE TOWN just outside the northern apex of the
Camargue, where the two arms of the Rhône divide for the
final journey southwards, is every inch a Provençal town. It
still bears the marks of its Greek and Roman history; the Greek
influence less obviously in the faces of its people, the Roman
influence most obviously in the ruins and remains of arena,
thermal baths and ancient theatre. Its tiny stone-framed streets,
large main boulevard with Wednesday and Saturday markets
ablaze with colour, half-dead chickens and rabbits, are full of
contrast and give no warning of what the Camargue is like.
Except when, on Saturday mornings, Camargue ranchers sporting their horseman's hats and trousers are to be seen taking
*pastis* outside the pavement cafés. Arles is the Provence of sun
and flowers, the sweet smell of rosemary and thyme drying over
the centuries in the Alpilles, and the decaying stone that
reconstructs history for our memory banks. I think it is safe
to say that, after this heady introduction, the Camargue is
a disappointment to most first-time visitors. It is Provence
still, but the other side of the ancient coin. The Camargue
is the Provence of the peasant, where life is stark, simple
and more brutal than that sweet smell would ever dare to
tell.

Till recent decades, locals believed the Camargue could never
become a tourist attraction. They knew its superficial horrors.
It is flat and bleak, especially in winter. Some of its highest
points are the dunes westwards towards Aigues-Mortes. There
is a monotony of pale green and greys, as grass and scrubby

vegetation give way to relentless water and sky. Few trees break up the horizon. There are mosquitoes from June to September that pay no respect to human status or wealth. And the temperature can soar to the unmerciful hundreds in the summer, drying up much of the water. Horses and bulls suffer under scant, leafless trees, scratching away at flies till the blood oozes out. And in the winter, it freezes. The *mistral* blows relentlessly. Locals say it only lets up for four days in the year (though statistics show its yearly average is two hundred and eighty days) and wryly point out that without it there would be mushrooms on the walls. The *mistral* is a drying wind, the *mangeo-fangeo* (mud-eater) of Provence. It makes people bad-tempered and, some say, suicidal. It gets into the head like an automatic drill.

Lawrence Durrell, who has lived just north of the Camargue for fifteen years, wrote in his travel essays, *Spirit of Place*, that to him the Camargue was like Argentina, a country he had not liked very much. "Here it is still eighty years behind the times and the nearness of Little Argentina [the Camargue] with its swamps, mosquitoes and wind should effectively drive off tourists for a while yet."

The Camargue hides its inhabitants well. But they are there all right, in their isolated farmhouses, living a life that is of their own, if not always of an enviable style. The Camargue is the kind of place that throws up characters of no mean size. It has a strangely varied indigenous population including weathered farm workers; hunters; fishermen; poachers and shepherds; the rich agricultural farmers, and the not so rich but eternally aristocratic breeders of bulls and Camargue horses; the flamboyant horsemen and women and the erratic young men who live to tempt their fate with the wild nature of the Camargue bull. The history of the land and its people has led to the strange situation where, in this tract of largely uncultivatable ground, the whole is actually a patchwork of private properties where rights to entry are strictly regulated. That is why the Camargue at first looks rather like a police state with wire fencing and curt notices restricting the visitors to two main

roads. It is not always understood that you cannot wander at
will over the delta's deserted wastes.

The unobtrusive inhabitants live on large Provençal farms,
called *mas* or *domaines*, which themselves are protected from
view (but really from the *mistral*) by avenues of trees left
standing by thoughtful ancestors. There are one or two small
villages with a couple of shops in the northern part, but it is
only in the coastal towns that the numbers of people start to
increase. There are two main towns: eastwards, just by the
mouth of the Grand Rhône, is the industrial town of Salin-de-
Giraud. Not a pretty town, it was built at the end of the nineteenth century when the industrial demand for sodium chloride
increased rapidly and the salt company of Péchiney threw up
workers' housing. The town has one salt works and one
chemical works and its housing could have been modelled on
a row of tenements in Salford. It is empty apart from two huge
bars with their pool rooms. There is hardly a French person
living there as most of the labour is imported from Spain and
Morocco. Westwards, in sharp contrast, is the other town. The
once fishing village of Les-Saintes-Maries-de-la-Mer is now a
tourist town almost on the scale of the Côte d'Azur. Its houses
are white-painted, Mediterranean-style and there are narrow
streets crammed with boutiques and souvenir shops. It is cold
or windy for much of the year, and here again French people
are in a minority.

And it is Moroccan or Spanish labour that is mostly seen
working in the fields of the Camargue, too. Despite contrary
appearances, the area has always had some bonuses for those
who own the land, but it never became popular as a place to
live and work in, and the population has remained stable at
about eight thousand for many years. Farming has always been
carried out by the landowning families, using immigrant labour
in spring and autumn. The *mas* are designed for that way of life,
with the main farmhouse flanked by outhouses and bunk-houses.

Temporary workers are never going to be the happiest
residents, and the Moroccans, particularly those who now come
in via Marseilles and stay for a month or two, are still not

totally accepted by the French natives, the full-time field workers who call themselves proudly *paysans*. For these peasants money can be earned in summer and eked out over the winter. It is for them that the delta's bleak and wintery face is probably hardest. Living in the Camargue is like living on an island: you are cut off by the twenty-five-mile journey to nearby Arles, and without a car you are trapped. Working and living on some *mas* you may be twenty miles from the nearest café, bar, or shop. It can be a lonely life. There are faces and eyes around that might have caught the tortured vision of Van Gogh had he stayed longer in Arles. They speak of the subtle cruelty of the natural world. The hunters, fishermen or horsemen who meet on Friday evenings in the large, draughty bars, drink *pastis* and play cards, know the silence of all the other evenings spent alone. That is why Camarguais are so good at celebrating, and inventing occasions for celebration.

And, in this sense, it is much the same for the delta's aristocrats: the wealthy farmers or proud stockbreeders. Memories recall Saturday journeys to Arles on horseback when provisions for the week were bought, not only for the family, but for all the farmworkers too: *saucisson d'Arles* (the rich sausage made of bull meat), olives, fruit and grain were bought by the sack or barrel load. Olive oil was brought round to the *mas* by the barrel. But the trip to Arles, at the turn of the century, was such an effort and such an occasion for festivity that many rich families kept a town house and stayed over until Sunday. In the first decades of this century, a small railway line ran between Arles and the two main routes to Salin-de-Giraud and Les-Saintes, stopping at all the major *mas* and acting as a lifeline. Sadly, the introduction of the car led to a premature end to the small-carriaged, open-topped, three-car train, heated by paraffin stove and with a personality all of its own. The old stations can still be seen in some places.

Farming on a Camargue *mas* is big business, and as the land has been passed on through the generations, marriages have linked up many of the families into joint ownership. The houses, which were mostly built during the eighteenth and nineteenth centuries, are graceful, cool and perfectly structured on three sides of a rectangle round a yard. They stand alone but for the cover of trees, like strange visitors in this landscape, resolutely keeping out the dread mosquitoes and backed sourly to the dominant wind. Many of the houses proudly display the beautiful Provençal-style of long dining room, imposing table (some, twenty-four feet long), the bread cupboard on the wall, rich, dark-wood furniture and cool, tiled floor. There is usually a welcome for a friend, time to stop and share a drink, a habit learned from long weeks of solitariness; a stranger may even become a friend if he or she is the first visitor for a long time. And around the table the families still talk with regret of the slow passing of this way of life, which can seem depressing to an outsider, in its isolation and dependence on other members of the family.

Something like half of the owners of the *mas* are not farmers in the usual sense, struggling with the vagaries of wheat, rice, fruit or vines, but the members of a unique band of ranchers known as *manadiers*. As the small black bull of the Camargue was hiding in the marshes before man settled, it is hardly surprising that before long man should have found a way of exploiting him. The Camargue bull is different from the Spanish strain in character and personality—a difference which led to its own unique usage at the *course libre*. There are some forty or fifty *manades* (ranches which specialise in breeding bulls for the *course*) in the Camargue, whose owners are colourful local figures and whose life's work is a passion. They employ their own version of cowboy/ranch-hand, called *gardians*, whose traditional home is a reed hut, *cabane*, found alone in the marshes where in times past the cowboy would eat, sleep and eke out his weird existence.

*Gardians* are now more likely to live at the *mas*, or to be a friend of the *manadier*, who will come from his home in a nearby town to help out during the busy seasons. For the old-style *gardians*, popular though the idea may be, are hard to come by these days, and usually it is the *manadier* and his sons or nephews who ride out early in the mornings to check that their stock, which lives in a semi-wild state, has not been injured. Other work involves moving the animals to new pasture ground and choosing which beast should go into the arena and which should go to the abattoir.

It was one local rancher and personality, Denys Colomb de Daunant, who helped to immortalise the Camargue and its way of life. Colomb de Daunant is an archetypical *manadier* and a talented photographer. Appreciating the beauty of his own environment, he collaborated with writer and film maker Albert Lamorisse and together they made the famous film *Crin Blanc* in 1953, about a boy and a wild horse in the wild Camargue. This was over twenty years ago and it is since then that the face of the delta has changed. Not just because of the film, of course. The film speaks romantically about a deserted country where herds of wild bulls and horses roam free. It presents the *gardians* and *manadiers* as men devoted to a lifetime in the wild, suffering losses in their stock through cold and drowning and making purely spiritual gains.

Folco, the young boy in the film, was played by Alain, who still lives in the Camargue though he works in Marseilles. That film had a subtle effect on every Camarguais' life. Colomb de Daunant runs one of the largest ranching-style hotels, Mas de Cacherel, where holidays include bed, board and horse rides. He is one of the most respected of the *manadiers* and rides up front with the top three whenever the horsemen of the Camargue are on show. For younger people, like Alain, the nostalgia whipped up by the film is not totally convincing. Some of the young people follow the customs of the Camargue and keep up the traditions. Others treat them as anachronisms and look to the Camargue simply as a quiet retreat.

To some, the life of the *gardian* lends itself to open mockery in its earnest following of a way of life of a century ago. The poor, simple and earthy life of the cowboy does not really fit into today's realities. But then for a lot of Camarguais the passions involved are more than just nostalgia, they are deeply emotional and almost genetic. And for many, the very real financial problems posed by such an old-fashioned way of life

Salicornia and dead tamarisk tree in the *sansouire* region

Evening light over the Étang de Vaccarès

have been answered in part by tourism. So, you find one-time horsemen, unable to support a family on the pay of ranchhand-cum-cavalier, turning to managing hotels that specialise in these horse rides. He may make sure that the bar of the hotel looks out over the corral, as horses are still his passion. And, while the *manadiers* are lively local personalities, unless they can depend on a private fortune, you may find that the property is owned by some industrialist or wealthy Frenchman.

These associations seem to be successful and enable the Camarguais to keep a semblance of independence. Such is the fantastic story of the *manades* that when the archivist Gerard Gadiot was writing a book on the folklore, he included a map of the area marking every *manade* and its owner. Through marriage or financial alignments, most are shared between three or four families. Notably, the great *pastis*-making company of Ricard from Marseilles, owns the huge and historic Mas Méjanes (now a ranching hotel) plus others nearby. Four *manades* are jointly owned by Camarguais Marcel Mailhan, head of the Association de Chevaux de Race Camargue, and François Fabre, wealthy politician and friend of the late President Pompidou. Similarly, *manadier* Hubert Yonnet, from one of the oldest families of the Camargue, and president of the ancient Confrérie de Gardians, is strictly speaking manager of a herd of Spanish strain bulls (reared for the *corrida*) for the great Salins du Midi company who lease him the land. Locals do not think of it that way, however, for the *manadier* has the skill and that is more important than the industrialist's money. But a lot of properties were bought up in this way after the War when land was at a premium. Yet the original *manadiers* and ancient owners of the *mas* stick to their property with all the pride and independence of the old separate state of Provence, as well as the pride of the Camargue.

I am a romantic myself which is maybe why I love the Camarguais so much. They are unashamedly so. They are very openly aware of their environment. They know that their countryside may appear flat and dull to the outsider, sensationalised by flashes of pink from the Flamingoes, of white from the horses and black from the bulls. But if you see somebody standing by the Étang de Vaccarès at six in the evening just gazing as the grey sea and sky blend into no horizon, or on the dykes by the sea watching the Flamingoes flying in from their breeding grounds to take shift work in the breeding colony's crèche, it needn't be a tourist lost on his way home, it is just as likely to be a *manadier* or a farmer or a hotel manager, thinking, if only we could fly so easily.

The Camargue is quiet, except for a buzz of cars. And it is lonely. The atmosphere, described by every writer, has always been one of sadness. Henri Bosco spoke in his novel, *Malicroix*, of "this country of sadness". Joseph D'Arbaud's beast in *La Bête du Vaccarès*, talks of "my peacefulness and my sad happiness". It's an area that gives birth and support to loners. There are those born to the way of life and those who have come to seek it out. The farmers and ranchers have it in their bones, but the ornithologists, naturalists and scientists who spend long days and nights in the marshes are attracted by the solitariness of this timeless land as much as by the unique flora and fauna. Sometimes, for those who become adopted Camarguais, the flatness, the bleakness and the monotony turn themselves into hostile images and newcomers speak of their depression on arrival. They also speak, though, of the change in them—that leads to a fear that they might one day have to leave. It's a place that gets its hooks into people.

# Chapter 2

## BULL GAMES

---

HUNDREDS OF PEOPLE were in the streets, at least a third of them on horseback. The usual kind of riding gear was on parade, but the horse-riders themselves had their own particular style. The men were in grey or beige moleskin trousers narrowed at the ankle, black velvet jackets, white frilled shirts and wide-brimmed hats. They had tiny spurs on their boots and *tridents* over their shoulders (the *trident* is a long pole with a three-forked prong at the end). Some were carrying women *en croupe*, sidesaddle behind them; women who themselves were dressed in traditional Arlesienne costume of long skirt, and crossed over bodice of muslin and lace, like a delicate version of the Welsh dress. The occasion could have been one of many. Like the day of the horse in Les-Saintes-Maries-de-la-Mer where the local *gardians* and *cavaliers* amuse themselves in the arena; or the day of the *gardians* in Arles, the biggest event when traditions are brought out from behind a screen and given public exposure. Or, just one of the hundreds of *courses libres* which take place during the summer months and which may be preceded by an *abrivado* when the bulls are let free in the streets, frantically chased by *gardians* at full gallop and young boys on foot, who steer the bulls back into the *toril*—the bulls' enclosure at the arena. Whatever the day, Camarguais seem to have occasions like this written into their consciousness. It's *la fé di biou* (the passion for bulls) celebrated in public spectacle.

To understand the Camargue you have to come somewhere near understanding the rôle of the bull. He is king and idol. King of the arena and pride of place in the people's hearts. The art of *tauromachie*, espoused and elevated by writers like Hemingway and Henri de Montherlant, doesn't bear much relation. By comparison to the *machismo* of the Spanish bull-fight, the Provençal bull game is almost emasculated. Which is why, for so many, particularly for squeamish visitors from the northern countries, the Provençal bull game is such a joy.

Firstly, the bull is not killed. It leaves the arena at the end of the day as it came in—through the *toril* and then goes back to the plains. The bulls often live to a great age, sometimes to twenty or twenty-three years, and not only are they constantly talked about, but they are quite genuinely loved. There is no blood during a bull game (unless from an accident to one of the men in the ring). Yet man is still pitting his wits against the bull. At the *course libre*, the bulls are known as *cocardiers*. They storm into the ring, one at a time, wearing a red rosette (*cocarde*) between the horns, two *glands* (white wool tassels) on the horns and two *ficelles* (strings) around the base of the horns. The idea is that instead of one toreador making passes, the ring is open to anyone brave or foolish enough. This total openness, which is what the name implies, can lead to chaos in the ring and more generally the *course* is run with a team of up to twenty men, known as *razeteurs*, whose task it is to get as near the bull's horns as possible, and to snatch the rosette or strings using the comb called a *crochet* or *razet*. The whole game is skilled, breathtaking and dangerous. As the *razeteurs* make their runs, and, chased by the bull, leap into the air over the wooden barrier stopping only to brush their feet against the wood, finally coming to a halt with their hands against the concrete balustrade, the whole scene is less Hemingwayesque than Chaplinesque. It's an afternoon's entertainment in the hot sun, as is the *corrida*, but the crowd isn't drawn there by the skill of the toreador at avoiding death or by the smell of blood. It has come for the laughs, the "oohs" and "ahs" of amazement. The tenacity of the bulls and the balletic leaps of the young men make it a stimulating experience.

It is the *manadiers* of the Camargue who bring their bulls along to any of the arenas in the hinterland, for the Camargue itself

only has two towns large enough to support an arena—Les-
Saintes and Salin-de-Giraud. But the way of life of the *manades*
and the *course libre* extends beyond the Camargue to all the little
towns and villages in the north-east and north-west of Provence:
up to Avignon, across to Aigues-Mortes and to Fos-sur-Mer. Each
town has its own arena holding from between two thousand to
five thousand people. Sometimes, a large splendid *course libre*
will be held in the twenty-six thousand seat arena at Arles or
Nîmes, but usually those high numbers are only drawn in for
the *corrida* (*mis-à-mort*) which takes place a few times during
the summer.

The *course libre* is essentially a small, local sport, rather like
the local football or cricket team. It is not a particularly lucrative business and the *manadiers* lease the arena from the munici-
pality so it is their responsibility to arrange for bulls and
*razeteurs*. Obviously, the pluckier and smarter the bull, the
better the crowd. The skill of the *razeteur* will also influence
the size of the audience, but on the whole it's the bull that
draws the crowd. The *manadier* takes the gate money; the
*razeteur* is playing for money prizes put on the *cocardes*. These
are small sums put up by local shopkeepers and restaurateurs:
all of it a mixture of advertising and goodwill.

In a small arena, like the one to the north of Arles, at
Fontvieille (near Daudet's windmill), a crowd of perhaps two
thousand pours into the arena on one of the first spring days in
May. The *mistral* has just let up after a week of solid blowing
and the crowd relaxes at the promise of yet another Provençal
summer. The bulls are waiting in the *toril*, a wooden enclosure
with a platform of planks above the bulls' heads where the
*gardians* can walk and handle them. The bulls are tied by the
horns to the platform, so the *gardians* can attach the *cocardes*.
Sometimes, at more homely occasions, the bulls' horns are
capped with a metal thimble-like cover.

The tension mounts as the seats fill up. Men behind micro-
phones sit above the *toril* and all eyes are fixed on the wooden
door. Spanish music is coming over the loudspeaker and
*razeteurs* waiting to make their entrance limber up in the

corridor behind the barrier. At the sound of "Carmen", the ten top *razeteurs* who are competing for points in a league prize, march proudly into the arena to take their applause, like a football team on parade. They are dressed more like tennis players, from a decade ago, in long white trousers and white T-shirts. Then they return behind the barrier, while the *toril* door is lifted, and a steaming, angry-looking beast storms into the arena, charges round a few times clearly wondering how he's going to get out again.

The Camargue bull is smaller in stature than his Spanish brother. But the most obvious difference is in his horns, which curve upwards like a lyre, rather than outwards. To charge, like the Spanish bull, he would have to get his head right down. But then he would be unlikely to do that, anyway, for his temperament is totally different. Basically, he's afraid and wants to get away, but if he's in a corner he'll do his best to attack with his horns. He's quick-footed, intelligent and a fast thinker—which makes him all the more exciting. There are accidents between *razeteur* and bull; some say too many. One man was suspended completely off the ground with the bull's horn poking through his arm. If the *razeteur* is trapped before the barrier, a common mishap is for the horns to rip the back of his shirt, or worse, to penetrate his back or thigh. Accidents, amazingly, are not feared. Volle, a *razeteur* who is *gardian* at the Mas les Marquises (one of the biggest *manades* of bulls), is proud of his twenty-eight wounds.

The bull is given a few minutes to pace round the arena working out his pitch while the *razeteurs* study his form. What kind of bull is he? Fast and nimble or slow and blundering? Intelligent or a bit dim? They work out their play. Then they begin. At a run, a *razeteur* will come up from behind along the left side of the bull, trying, as he runs across the animal's path, to snatch one of the *cocardes*. They have to be taken in the correct order, and first to go is the rosette. The *razeteur* is moving at speed, throwing his hand out behind him, which, if his timing is right, will hit the bull between the horns as his flight path and the bull's thundering path coincide. If he doesn't get the turn right, he finds the bull on his tail and his only course is to fly the barrier. Sometimes, the bull, caught in mid-motion and angered by the nifty disappearance of this interfering man, will charge at the barrier, crashing his horns against the wooden planks and, lifting the pieces of wood out of their sockets, toss them mercilessly into the air. The audience loves it.

They love it even more if he's the firebrand type and hurls himself over the barrier, following the white streak of man. Any humans standing behind the barrier leap smartly over it back into the arena while others grab hold of rails above them and swing above the bull's head, and those of the audience, whose feet are dangling over the side, hastily draw them in. Some bulls, like the massive ten-year-old Goya, the star from the Mas les Marquises, owned and bred by *manadier* Henri Laurent, become the favourite of the *piste* (ring). Goya knows neither fear nor shame and jumps the barrier as if he were a *razeteur*.

After fifteen minutes, "Carmen" strikes up, the *toril* door is opened and the bull, with or without all his *cocardes*, is expected to leave. If he won't go out, another smaller bull is often sent in to draw him out.

If to the uninitiated the whole spectacle looks like a farce and an undisciplined riot, then a few more attendances and some study of the local magazine *Le Camariguo*, which follows the *course*, may open your eyes and make the sport much more interesting. For the *razeteurs* are very skilled and are controlled by strict rules. Their trade has to be learned as much as any other form of *tauromachie*. The *razeteurs'* conduct in the ring is strictly watched. Their dress has to conform; their T-shirts must carry no advertising, and they must not wear any head-gear, towels, scarves or handkerchiefs.

One of the problems with the Camargue bull is that, in his distaste for being in the ring, he finds his own spot, known as the *querencia*, which is on the left-hand far side of the arena. The *querencia* is often not as rounded as the opposite side and once the bull puts himself there, he won't budge. No *razeteur* is allowed to take the *cocardes* from an unmoving bull—nor would he want to, so the bulls often have to be goaded into action.

There are certain older men, ageing *razeteurs* who can no longer take the strain of stardom and the risks of the game, whose job it is to cry, "Hey! Taureau!" in the hope of persuading the beast into some action. Once the bull is on the move again, the next problem for the *razeteur* is posed by his team mates. With some ten or twelve in the league and in fierce competition, getting themselves and the bull in the right place for a calculated move is not easy. So, in fact, the *razeteurs* work in teams with older, or maybe apprentice, *razeteurs*, called *tourneurs*. It is these men who try to make the bull run in a certain direction so that their *razeteur*, priming himself to spring into action, will be aiming in the right direction. The *cocarde*, or rosette, always goes first, and is the easiest as it is perched precariously between the bull's horns. It carries less money and less points for the league. After the rosette, it's the turn of the two *glands* and then the two *ficelles*. These last strings are the hardest as they are seemingly attached by elastic. They have first to be cut and then snatched off. This is the time when rows break out as often enough a good *razeteur* will manage to loosen them, his *tourneur* will fail to aim the bull his way and along comes another *razeteur* who walks off with the trophy. It has led to fights between men in the ring before now—as money, prestige and pride are all at stake.

The prize money grows in one, two, and five pound stakes which are continuously announced over the loudspeakers as the good local people offer their rewards. An average *razeteur* could take home twenty to thirty pounds from an afternoon while the champion for the day will claim a few hundred usually donated by Ricard who sponsor the *courses*. The good *razeteurs* also receive tips from the *manadiers* (it's to their benefit to get the most skilful human performers to complement the daring of their bulls). In fact, you might see some *razeteurs* sitting a bull out—if he doesn't approve of the *manadier*'s lack of generosity.

Six bulls and the afternoon is over; but they will have been a carefully balanced group of six different kinds of bulls for better viewing. During the interval while the toreador music is playing, the local kids run on to the *piste* playing at bull and man, which resembles our game of tag. It is interesting to watch a group of Spanish kids and a group of Provençal kids at the same time. They play a totally different game as if by instinct. The first group are intent on charging, the second on chasing. The Provençal bull game is more than a custom; it's a whole way of life.

When a Camargue bull puts his head out of the *toril* into the arena as a three-year-old, in Camarguais a *ternen*, it may be the first time he has smelt or sensed man's presence apart from one earlier memorable and traumatic occasion. For the Camargue bull lives in the wild, on the salty plains, finding his own food and shelter, growing up unfussed over and without restrictions. But, as an *anouble*, a yearling, he did have to face man in no uncertain manner. The occasion is that known as a *ferrade*, or branding. It's a ritual that can be traced back to the Minoan culture of Crete, whose sport of bull-leaping was chronicled on their coins and pottery. The *ferrade* of the Camargue involves similar gestures. The bull is tackled and grappled, by hand; its horns are caught, the tail is held and the bull is firmly knocked over on to its side. The whole struggle turns into a very racy farce in which the man is dragged along by a frisky young bull. But he loves every minute of his contact with the wild, untameable animal.

It has been popularly held in the Camargue that these bull games go back not to the Minoan culture but to the pre-Christian Mithraic religion which came to France with the Romans, and was espoused particularly by the soldiers. The Persian god Mithra became a cult figure. He was a young hero, symbolising sun and energy, who made a ritual of slaughtering a bull representing man's control of the sources of energy and good. Mithraism is still seen as the source of the Provençal sports and worship of the bull. But on studying this, I found that the local archivist, Gerard Gadiot, author of an invaluable and incredibly detailed book, *En Camargue: Taureaux, Chevaux et Gardians*, had an even more fascinating and, to me, more convincing theory. It is the survival of the *ferrade*, in its unchanged form, which, he maintains, gives hints that the

Minoan or Cretan influence was actually the major influence, not Mithraism. Gadiot's evidence includes Greek coins showing very similar activities of bull-leaping and chasing in Minoan Crete. There are coins which show Thessalos taming a furious bull. He is running on the right of the bull and is travelling in the same direction, seizing the animal's horns in the same way today's *gardians* do. Another coin has on its front and back a horseman at gallop following a bull which again is one of the activities of a *ferrade*—the part known as the *triage*. Then a bas-relief at Smyrna shows five horsemen chasing three bulls. They seize the bulls by the horns, jump off the horse and throw the bulls over. All of which is still played out at *ferrades* all over the Camargue to this day.

The *ferrades* of today are hardly held as a conscious echo of ancient rites, culture or cult. They are the excuse for a day of spectacle, sport and fun; one of those occasions which, in the past, Camarguais dreamed up as a way of getting together, partly to help each other out with the branding and partly to ensure some good partying. *Ferrades* still take place on the *manades* from February to September; some are public, some private. This again is an instance of the Camarguais' instinct for self-preservation. For, although they need to be able to retain the original spirit for their own friends, they also need the income from paying visitors. So both sorts take place.

All over the area in the south of France, known as Provence and Languedoc, people with *la fé di biou* join *clubs taurins*. Small villages have their own clubs, meeting in the local café; others are larger and are sponsored by big companies like Ricard. To arrange a *ferrade*, the club makes contact with a *manade*. These days a *manadier* will divide up his stock taking, say, three or four *anoubles* from the herd to any one *ferrade*. It's a slow business anyway, but it also ensures that some are saved for another day and another show. It's at the *manadier*'s own private *ferrade* that the occasion has its original purpose—quite simply an occasion for a dance and a drink, while you show off your skill, courage and hospitality.

But, public or private, the traditional methods are still used, and modern life has introduced no short cuts. The *ferrade* begins with a *triage* when the bulls are chosen from among the *anoubles* in the herd, and forced away from their mothers. About a dozen *gardians* may be involved; not all are employees of the *manadier*, but may be friends and neighbours who love nothing better than getting on a horse and lending a hand. They use the *trident* to nudge the young bull away, and with a cry chase him either over the flat plains to an open fire in the centre of the scrub, or down a wooden fenced corridor into the *bouvau*, or small corral. Wherever the bull ends up, he first has to be caught. Three or four of the *gardians* jump off their horses and run round or up behind the bull. Someone, at some point, has to take hold of the horns, and is usually dragged along by the bull. Another *gardian* helps him to throw the *anouble* on to its side. Its legs are held together and roped with a lasso, the head is held down and the *manadier* comes over from the fire with the white-hot branding iron ready. There's a burning smell, a groaning bellow from the animal and the iron is taken off. The *manadier* usually brands with three numerals and his own mark, which is rather like a family crest. The final pain for the animal is known as the *escoussure*, when its ears are nicked, again with the mark of the *manade*.

Then the *gardians* steel themselves while the animal is let free. It jumps up, looks round and aims for the nearest way out. If the *ferrade* is for paying guests who want to share some of the thrills, they often get a desperate *anouble* aimed at them. People sometimes get thrown this way, but the animals are still small and it's unlikely to be dangerous. And anyway, such is the love of the bull games that any onlooker would be proud to display the wounds received from a bull. Or, if the *ferrade* is private, in the *manade*'s own *bouvau*, the *gardians* may keep the bull in the corral while they besport themselves awhile. It is a young bull's first training for the *course*, and may be his first realisation that, with the often drunken crowd of would-be *gardians*, man isn't always so clever. But that's the fascination of the game. The bull is not stupid and by the time he's a three-year-old he may have developed a lively intelligence as well as sprightly feet and a quiet understanding that he has got to play the game.

It's a bull's indifference that really gets a Provençal crowd going and the shouts of "Hey! Taureau!" resound around the *bouvau* as the intrepid young men, and in this case, women, pit their wits and strength against the bull's. It's the same game as that played at the more sophisticated *course libre*. But by this time they have lunched and are helped by *pastis*. For them it's an adventure never to be forgotten. Sometimes the northerner from Paris, or visitor from Britain, looks on with horror at the humiliation apparently suffered by the bull. But the Provençal admiration and respect for the bull, not to mention love, has to be borne in mind. The bull seems to get the last laugh on most occasions.

Yet, when Alexandre Dumas visited the south of France as one of the first tourists and wrote up his travels in 1851, he was none too pleased with the spectacle. He wrote: "There a sort of butcher of Herculean fame awaited them; and taking the bull by the horns, depressing one and raising the other, he threw him on his side". Dumas reported witnessing the horrifying show of ill-treatment of the bull, *gardians* abusing the animal with the *trident* and one poor bull even getting the three-pronged fork up his nostrils. But Dumas's visit was prior to the awakened sensibility that came with the early part of this century. The ancient and revered traditions could well have degenerated to something akin to butchery. By contrast, today's young *gardian* will adamantly maintain that, while he may be blood-spattered from nicking the bull's ears, he loves the whole sport of playing and testing himself against the bull's superior strength and size with such a passion that harm to the bull is the last thing he envisages. There is nothing better to the Provençal caught with *la fé* than the thrill of the chase, where man after all is the one who is being hunted but, he hopes, hunted within a situation which he can control and readily escape.

From the records in Arles, the existence of the *ferrade* and of the sport with wild animals can be traced right through Provençal history. Things are indeed tame these days compared

with former bloodthirsty pursuits. The first document to
mention bull games is dated 1222. Then in 1402, the memoirs of
a Bernard Boisset record that King Louis set a lion against a bull
in Arles, and the bull won. In 1551, though, a gentleman of
Arles, Pierre Quiqueran de Beaujeu, wrote an extremely
important chronicle of everyday life in Provence called
*Provence Louée* on which historians of the area have to rely. He
wrote of the fury of the bulls and he mentioned that there were
sixteen thousand of them in the Camargue: "Just as their
number is large, so is their temper."

Quiqueran de Beaujeu, in his long and detailed description
of the *ferrade*, could be describing an event that happened yesterday. He tells how they get the bulls to the fire. He describes
the feast and the use of the bull as after-dinner recreation.
It's very solid evidence that the traditions haven't changed. In
1622, Louis XIII came to Arles and wanted to be taken to an
arena to see the Camargue bulls. In 1780, in a work called
*Voyage Littéraire de Provence*, Arles was described as the town
where you find the most traces of ancient customs. In 1813, an
Arlesian writer called Pierre Véran wrote that he found great
pleasure in the spectacle of an animal hitting a man who is
irritating him. He did not like to see a tragic death but if a man
has been lured by a sum of money to take on the bull then his
first instinct would be to laugh. By the late eighteenth century,
the arenas of Provence had all been blocked up as the *courses*
were forbidden. But, by 1813, Véran was describing the best
*ferrade* he had ever seen, the type that hadn't taken place since
1760. He counted more than five hundred and thirty-two
wagons, six hundred horses, one hundred bulls and six thousand
people.

I doubt if you would ever find six thousand people at any one
*ferrade* any more, but the occasion for making the branding into
a feast survives. At a private *ferrade* organised by a local *club
taurin* you might find the whole village has taken the day off
work. This is their annual jamboree. It's a day of *pastis*, an
open-air banquet, of music, dancing and sporting with bulls.
And it's something the tourist cannot be a part of. The day

begins with a rendezvous at the favourite café, and by mid-morning cars have all piled into the *manade*'s grounds. The food is stored under trees. Crates of wine, and boxes of *saucisson d'Arles* are ready for the eating. The morning is taken up with the *triage*, catching the bulls and branding them. Then there's a dive for the *pastis* wagon, serviced by a barrel of water. People are thrown into *roubines* (irrigation channels) and fireworks crackle in hat brims and under feet. They certainly let their hair down, if not burn it up. Someone lights a fire, and the meat is grilled—so much meat! The wine is opened and they sink on to the grass to devour a meal of Tom Jonesian proportions. When the band strikes up with "Carmen", the revellers stir themselves to jump round and round on the stubbly grass.

In the afternoon, after the branding, the two and three-year-olds are brought in as recreation and the drunken and unwise run around with them, incredibly energetic in the face of sun, food and wine. The day, it has to be said, finishes with a *pastis*-bar-crawl home. Not everybody in the Camargue likes a *ferrade* but for those who do it is a very special way of life and a fascinating reflection on the past.

*Chapter 3*

## A MECCA FOR ORNITHOLOGISTS

---

BLACK SHAPES WHEELING across an empty sky, gracefully arched necks craning into a sunset, the harsh cries of hovering mother feeding young, the nervous chatter of young birds before a storm or their happy frolicking after a *mistral*—all are well known sights or signals to the vast numbers of amateur and professional ornithologists who visit or work in the Camargue. And the number of cars or vans that stop suddenly in the middle of the road, as wild-eyed enthusiasts jump out clutching binoculars and note pad, bear witness to the fact that half of the annual pilgrims come to the Camargue for the bird life.

It's a busy feeding and breeding ground and one of the most important wetland zones in Europe; and it is full of distinctive birds not seen in northern Europe. It is, for instance, the most northerly place where Flamingoes not only feed but breed. The Camargue has been a happy hunting ground for ornithologists, particularly the British, since the Second World War. Yet, surprisingly, its secrets were unknown to the outside world for centuries.

It was only in 1946 that G. K. Yeates published his diaries of ornithological trips to Spain and the south of France and wrote, in *Bird Life of Two Deltas*, that, "a European bird trip is a very necessary stage in the development of a British ornithologist, if he is to get in proper proportion a panorama of the bird-life of his own islands". He describes with uncontrolled pleasure his findings: "I saw a Cock Redstart, a *phylloscopus* (Willow Wren I think), a Black-eared Wheatear, and most interestingly of all, an Ortolan Bunting. Glegg's list does not even mention this species for the delta." Until that time, the main works of reference by a British writer was W. E. Glegg's *Birds of l'Isle de la Camargue and the Petite Camargue* of 1931 and 1941. Yeates was amazed by the quality and quantity on show for the ornithologist, particularly the Flamingoes. On a third flying visit, he had been inspired to travel straight down to the Camargue from Yorkshire, having received a letter from a friend telling him, "Flamingoes started on April 14th to set up house on same old site using their old nests . . . six thousand birds . . . in the final throes of courtship and there there are up to now about a thousand eggs". Yeates, wife and colleague, were on the train the next day to be met in Arles by their friend with the greeting, "Englishmen, I presume". All sense went to the wind for Yeates. "The mention of Bee-eaters on telephone wires put an end to all talk of unpacking . . . not even a child with a box of crayons, a painting book, and a fertile imagination would ever evolve a more vivid creature than this brilliant bird which Nature has created. . . ." I know what he meant. Once you start seeing prolific numbers of gaily painted Bee-eaters, who still sit on telephone wires, you feel spoiled somehow.

It was in 1948 that Luc Hoffmann (now Vice-President of the World Wildlife Fund) first visited the Camargue as a student and was so taken by the bird life that he decided to stay. He bought and set up the Tour du Valat *mas* as an independent research station with one assistant. His fascination with the intricate pattern of flora and fauna was such that he embarked on several years of bird ringing to get to know the visitors a little better and to find out why they came. The Tour du Valat has been ringing an average of twenty thousand birds a year, their busiest time being in the spring when the birds are newly hatched. From recoveries in other countries they can follow their visitors' routes. They also do regular counts of the wintering ducks, counting them feeding and flying. The research station is now an international organisation of considerable repute: and Dr Hoffmann, as both biologist and conservationist, represents the Camargue at international conferences.

Many distinguished naturalists and ecologists have worked with Hoffmann, passing through the Camargue, or staying there to help them in their work. The Tour du Valat has a fund of information and data about bird populations and migrations which they are now beginning to use for further scientific research.

To introduce the bird population at this point is not the easiest thing for me. I will be honest and confess that before going to the Camargue I could only just recognise a London Sparrow (and then it had to be in London). But it's not hard to become an enthusiast. All you need is the use of another pair of eyes: ones that have been trained to be open and perceptive. That way it's like entering into a new, and almost fairy tale, world; it's like having your eyes washed clean or your consciousness awakened to a whole new pattern of images and colours.

For that reason I will put you in the hands of John Walmsley, one of the two Englishmen working at the Tour du Valat. Lancashire born and bred, John came to the Camargue as an ornithologist and has already stayed seven years. He is known locally (or at least ironically to himself) as *l'homme des marais*, as he spends long days and nights trudging through the marshes ringing the young birds and making a census of the nesting colonies of Grey and Purple Herons. Spring is his busiest time, of course, and by September 1974 he had already ringed some seven hundred and twenty-five young Purple Herons and fifty young Grey Herons. On one particular spring day he was travelling round a representative area of the Camargue, and the air was full of *mistral*. He was going out to an *étang* near the coast where his English colleague, Alan Johnson, from Nottingham, had seen a Wilson's Phalarope that same morning. If he could corroborate Alan's find, then there would really be something to celebrate, as a Wilson's Phalarope had only been seen in the Camargue once before. And the sight of a new species was excuse enough for a bottle of champagne that evening.

Taking one of the old 2-CV vans from the station, John

explained that although the tarmac roads of the Camargue
are now as good as any in France (in Yeates's day all the roads
were dusty, or muddy, tracks), driving is still a novel experience.
His path often leads him off the made-up roads to muddy
stretches where two-foot craters are disguised as innocuous
puddles and long furrows need to be manœuvred with skill.
There are times, driving along the embanked causeways, when
you are bridging two furrows with nothing but a steep drop
into the *étangs* to make you concentrate. John was dressed for
the occasion in rubber boots, and wet-proof clothes, plus two
pipes, camera and binoculars. Leaving the Tour du Valat and
driving down the main road towards Salin-de-Giraud, and the
beach known as the Plage d'Arles, he began to point out
the bird life. Along the cultivated roadsides there are Redstarts,
Wheatears, the Black-eared Wheatear (*Oenanthe hispanica*), and
another form which has a black throat. A Woodchat Shrike
is perched on top of a tree. "There are so many birds around,"
explained John. "There must have been a fall of birds migrating
from Africa. They are all coming out because the grass has
just been cut here and there's plenty of food which they need
after the wind and the rain. I was out on the *digue* [dyke]
on the first of May when the *mistral* was very strong and
a Wheatear just came into my hands. It was exhausted with
flying into the Camargue in all that wind." As the road
progressed there were Corn Buntings and Ortolan Buntings,
Stonechat, Whitethroats, a Sub-Alpine Warbler and overhead,
wheeling in the distance, Black Kites, Black-headed Gulls and
Common Terns.

The ground was giving way to the *sansouire* pattern of *étangs*
divided by dry, scrubby tracts of land. At the beach, John met
up with Alan who was gazing wistfully out to the Étang de
Grande Palun where he had earlier seen the Wilson's Phalarope.
"It's not there any more," he said. "All the water levels have
changed so much with that rain this morning." But, if the new
bird wasn't showing itself, there were breeding colonies of
Little and Common Terns on an islet in the middle of the
*étang*; also breeding colonies of Black-headed Gulls and the

ubiquitous Herring Gulls all round. By the stony edges of the *étang*, there were numerous Kentish Plovers, which lay their three eggs in a shallow dug-out among the pebbles. Then John trained his eye on four small birds as brown as the mud they hopped about in. They were Little Stints and Temminck Stints. Avocet were flying overhead with the high cry of, "keep, keep", in harmony with the Common Tern's sharp bark and loud, "kyark, kyark". The *étangs* also abound with Shelduck, Mallard, Marsh Harriers, Kestrels, Oystercatchers, Common Sandpipers, Black-tailed Godwits, Black-winged Stilts and the less familiar Knot and Redshank.

From the Plage d'Arles, John continued out along the *digue* to where a guard watches the Flamingo colony. As this breeding season coincides with the onset of the tourist season the guard stays day and night, armed with a telescope, to make sure the Flamingoes are not disturbed by the over-zealous photographers and keen ornithologists.

To get to the *digue*, John had to traverse back through the salt-producing town of Salin-de-Giraud, and on the way pointed to the common Little Egrets, much loved birds of the Camargue, and to the less common Cattle Egrets that are found only where bulls are grazing. Back among the tree-lined roads, the car skidded to a halt. "Look at that! It's *Monticola saxatilis*. Now that is exciting—a Rock Thrush. Look at its blue head and orange breast. A really beautiful bird and the first of the year. And there, just behind it, on that tree is a Woodchat Shrike, *Lanius senator badius*. See if you can see its white wing bar. I don't think there is . . . no, it hasn't got one. That's a strange sub-species. It must come all the way from Corsica to here, and back again. The Camargue is a great stopping-off place but usually for migrants from Africa and the southern Mediterranean, on their way north and returning."

The beautiful Purple Herons were seen hovering over marshy ground, the home of one of the colonies that John was systematically working his way through ringing and counting. Then more Mallard, "The female in front of the male. They always fly like that. That's another drake coming to join them. I've

seen as many as ten males following one female—though it is
the time of year of course." As he was driving on to the *digue*,
there rose out of the grey horizon a pink mist, a veritable
flash of colour from out of the dim light: the Camargue
Flamingoes.*

The Flamingoes' guard, another phenomenon of the Camargue, is Georges, a young boy from outside Arles, who spends
six months of the year in a lonely woodshed on the *digue*. His
hut, furnished in true Camargue style, has a mud floor, a small
frame bed, a few books, tiny kitchen and not much space.
Georges, who has a telescope for keeping an eye on the young
Flamingoes in the colony, is visited by the working ornithologists and also talks to the tourists who pass by and ask questions
(sometimes grotesque ones such as, "Are they geese?"). There
are over three thousand Flamingoes in the colony, but no one
will know till the nests are emptied how many are breeding
pairs, or from the eggshells how many young were born.
Flamingoes are a very unstable species as far as breeding goes.
They don't make great demands, ecologically speaking. They
need water to nest by, and an islet on which to build their mud-
pie style nests. They feed off brine shrimps (red in colour which
has led some people to surmise the origins of all Flamingoes'
rosy hue) and take it in turns to go into the Réserve lands to feed
and then return to look after the young in the crèche. As evening
fell, the Flamingoes began to return home in great numbers.
The noise from the colony of young is quite stupendous; but
who stops to notice that when the colour and sight of their
elders in flight is enough to set any sensitive soul on fire? This
year had been a momentous one for the ornithologists of Tour
du Valat, John explained, "The Flamingoes are moving on to
the *digue* now, which is incredible. We foresaw that because the
islet they nest on is getting too small and was overcrowded last
year. So we spent the winter making several hundred Flamingoes'

* For the information on the Camargue Flamingoes, I am indebted
to the paper written by Alan Johnson of the Tour du Valat:
"Camargue Flamingoes" (International Flamingo Symposium,
Slimbridge, July 1973).

nests to attract them from the islet to the new island. We made them just like you make sand castles—in buckets."

Viewing the Camargue Flamingoes through the telescope, or getting a camera angle on them overhead, one can understand the effect they have had on naturalists over the years. The adult, *Phoenicopterus ruber roseus*, is pale or bright pink, while the young is a sort of dirty brown. In the Camargue colony the year I was there, were also three birds of the Chilean variety who had escaped, perhaps from a zoo. These are smaller and rather comical-looking with their grey legs striped at the knee with a bright red band. And of course, a Flamingo in flight makes a photograph that drives people with cameras into a frenzy. The local ornithologists have had to persuade the Air Ministry to try to stop private, or military, low-flying aircraft flying over the Flamingoes—buzzing them to make them fly. They are easily panicked and take to the air without hesitation. Of course, people want to see the ease and grace with which they take off and keep on high, but the damage caused to the birds and their habits is inestimable.

In 1908, the naturalist F. M. Chapman wrote in *Camps and Cruises of an Ornithologist*: "There are larger birds than the Flamingo and birds with more brilliant plumage, but no other bird is so brightly coloured, and no other brightly coloured bird is so large. In brief, size and beauty of plume united reach their maximum of development in this remarkable bird. . . . When to these more superficial attractions is added the fact that little or nothing is known of the nesting habits of this singular bird, one may, in a measure at least, realise the intense longings of the naturalist, not only to behold a Flamingo City . . . but to lift the veil through which the Flamingo's home life has been dimly seen." In 1950, G. K. Yeates, on his second visit to the Camargue, wrote a book called *Flamingo City* and first used colour plates to capture the flight of this magnificent bird. Since that time, further work by ornithologists, such as those in the Camargue, has filled some of the gaps in the knowledge lamented by Chapman.

It now seems likely that Flamingoes were breeding in the area as far back as 1782 when the French naturalist Darluc mentioned them in his *Histoire Naturelle de Provence*. But to most people, they were a mystery and the colonies were not known about until 1947 when Étienne Gallett, an amateur naturalist and taxidermist from Arles, published his own work called *Les Flamants Roses de Camargue*. This chequered history is partly due to the long gaps of years when the Flamingoes have neither nested, nor bred, in the Camargue. This capricious nature is not easy to explain. It cannot be blamed on pollution fears, noise or nuisance worries. Ornithologists still have no answers though variations in the spring climate are now being studied. This year's breeding season comprised a colony of some three or four thousand. In December that figure would drop to a few hundred, and then by February again, when the influx starts, there are sometimes up to twenty thousand at any one time—most of which are just passing through.

On this windy, rainy day in May, out on the *digue*, John was surprised to see behind him a whole multitude of other little birds: a group made up of Wheatears, Whinchats, Pied Flycatchers, and Ortolan Buntings. "Just look at all those birds there on the road. There must have been a fall here this afternoon, probably brought down by the rain. It's incredible. There, as I said, you can see everything and anything in the Camargue. But don't think it's always like this. It's not every day you see this many birds." The Pied Flycatchers were feeding on evening clouds of *chironymides* and looking generally pleased at their safe arrival. Later that evening, another of John's colleagues reported seeing a Golden Oriole, and in the week that followed the trees and hedgerows became alive with Bee-eaters, Hoopoes, Rollers and Orioles, between them these are the most colourful birds to be seen. Bee-eaters after the fall were everywhere. Groups were silhouetted against the dark evening sky, their triangular shaped wings pinpointing them in a black-and-white photo finish. Seven or eight at a time would be seen sitting comfortably on one leafless tree, while Hoopoes flew down and, almost tame, would approach the stranger man for food.

But all that is nothing compared to the winter sight of the ducks. Then there are ducks everywhere, covering expanses of water in their thousands. In early July, for example, there will be between a thousand and fifteen hundred Teal (which is the most abundant species of the Camargue). In August, this figure goes up to around six thousand and then in November it reaches a platform of forty thousand individuals. (In December 1965 there were fifty-four thousand.) Apart from Teal, the Camargue also provides winter quarters for Mallard, Pintail, Gadwall, Widgeon, Shoveller, Pochard, Tufted Duck, Red-crested Pochard, Shelduck, Bewick Swans, Bean Geese, Coot and, of course, Flamingoes. In 1974, the figures for January and February showed a count of some one hundred and thirteen thousand ducks in January and an immediate sharp decrease to eighty thousand in February.

At times ornithologists get depressed that the results of ringing seem almost negligible. But they can say from the recoveries received that the Camargue's population of Teal fly south from Siberia, Northern Scandinavia and from Northern Russia. The biggest irony for the ornithologist is that most of their recoveries come from the deaths caused by shooting, not only in the Camargue but all along the birds' route. In the Camargue, the shooting season begins on 15th August until, for aquatic species, 31st March. Every year, around one hundred thousand ducks are killed; twenty thousand of these are Teal, the smallest and the ones that find it easiest to avoid the shot. The ducks aren't always as stupid as the hunters may think, though; they shelter on the protected marshes during the day and only leave for the feeding grounds in the evening. As the season progresses they learn how to fly higher above the range of the shot. Yet so many are still shot every year. The only mitigating factor is that total numbers of duck in the Camargue actually fluctuate. If hunting did suddenly stop, would anyone know what would happen if the feeding and breeding grounds then became overcrowded? As it is, from the high recovery returns—some thirteen per cent—information is available about the birds of the Camargue, information which is now being used in more intensive ecological surveys which ultimately should help to protect the wild life.

But there are other areas of the ornithologist's work in which the amateur, armed with gun or binoculars, cannot join. To make his census of the breeding colonies of the Purple and Grey Herons, for example, John Walmsley has to work through the marshes, ringing not only Herons but also any other breeding species (for all data is valuable). The Camargue's marshes are home not only to the associated colonies of Grey and Purple Herons, but to elusive Bitterns, to Gull-billed Terns, White-winged Black Terns, Whiskered Terns, Moustached Warblers, Marsh Harriers and Red-crested Pochard during the spring. So John's days are spent in the inhospitable marshes, knee or thigh deep in malodorous waters with flies, insects and dust from the reeds in his face, and squawkings of young birds in his ears. Perhaps not outwardly enviable, but to the ornithologist quite a natural way of life.

Armed for this work, John wears thigh-length *cuisses* (waders) and his oldest clothes. He also carries rings of pliable alloy, some pieces of cloth and a notebook and pen. He drives to the marsh in the middle of the Camargue, the evocatively named Marais de la Grand Mar which straddles the centre of the delta. He sets off down a mud path, past Egrets and Yellow Wagtails, following the large irrigation canal, Canal du Rousty, and leaves the car where there is a small flat-bottomed boat tied up by the edge of the marsh. The *barquette*, as it is known, is shared by hunter and ornithologist (this particular part of the marsh is owned by a private landowner as a hunting ground). The boat is moved, as with a punt, by a long pole with a forked end to grip the soft mud bottom of the marsh. Punting in the Camargue is known as *partaguer* and the boat slides over shallow empty waters between the jumps of tiny marsh-frogs and bubbles of freshwater fish gasping below. John guides the boat into the reeds, jamming it in place. He sets out on foot, finding his way through the thickset reeds, seemingly remembering his direction, and disappears for several hours.

Walking in the marshes is not easy; but it is something that all ornithologists in the Camargue have to get used to. Long strides take John from precarious reed platform to platform; the plants are pushed down to the sides making something firm for his feet to stand on. An experienced marsh walker does not leave an ugly trail behind him of broken reeds and crushed vegetation. There is nothing to hold on to for balance and one doesn't know if anything underfoot is stable either. The water may be knee deep or chest deep, which is something the inexperienced soon discovers.

There are hundreds of nests in the marshes, as the number of adults bringing food down to their young testifies: not to mention the noise coming from the empty mouths. But Heron nests are easy to miss, as they are in platforms of reeds constructed in the banks and well camouflaged by more, and more, reeds. But, in half an hour, John has found three nests, two Purple Heron's and one Grey Heron's (the Grey Heron's are the rarer). Suddenly, he comes across an elusive Bittern's nest, and is so thrilled at his find that he struggles back to the boat, and returns with a camera just to get a shot of the nest. The strangely ugly Bittern young, with pale orange feathers and very large, far too long, green legs, can only open their mouths and wail. But he takes hold of each one, and puts a ring over the tibia, just above the knee joint, gently prising it into a circular shape with the pliers, leaving enough room for the bird to grow. His first recovery from Nigeria this year, he says, is proof to him that he's a good ringer as it means the bird was able to fly that far.

None of the young has the beauty of its parents. The adult Purple Heron's flight path above the marsh exposes a flash of chestnut beneath a grey covering of feathers, and three yellow stripes. The heron is elegant and beautiful. The young are scrawny, scraggly and whining. Wading past nest after nest, John takes a broken leaf from a reed and places it over each nest he has ringed. Remarkably he doesn't lose sight or sense of direction, and he re-emerges later, very tired and very thirsty, to rush off and have a beer. But before he goes, there is a male Marsh Harrier flying overhead indulging in that complicated ritual of passing food to the female. The father brings the food, be it a snake or a frog, over the nest. The mother flies up to approach him and, at a certain point, as she wheels below him, the food is exchanged and elegantly caught by her talons.

*Chapter 4*

# A PATTERN OF ISLANDS

THE STORY OF Ducks and Flamingoes is, of course, telling us something else. The reason the Camargue is such a popular breeding and feeding ground for such a wide variety of species is that the vegetation of the delta is as distinctive and original as its more sensational visitors. Even someone with no botanical knowledge cannot help but notice the variety of habitat and the strange-looking plants, though they may feel it is surprising anything grows there at all. To gain any kind of understanding of the delta, we have to appreciate the rôle of salt and water in its formation. For the functioning of the delta rests on an intricate balance set up between salt, water and land.

The delta is affected by salt water from the sea and by fresh water from the rivers. The other main influences are the strong sea wind, the stronger land wind—the *mistral*—and the powerful summer sun. The south-easterly wind brings with it sea-water flooding so the salt content of the land is increased. The *mistral* makes the rivers overflow their banks and the salt is, to some extent, flushed out of the soil. During the summer, the shallow stretches of water, particularly in the more salty areas, evaporate under the sun and the earth is left parched and caked. But, of course, the extent of the salt concentration in both soil and water affects not only the kind of vegetation, but the species of birds that are attracted. Sea water, and salt, obviously have a stronger influence nearer the coast; fresh water and salt-free soil in the higher lands to the north of the delta. If we pan a camera over the whole of the delta, going into areas that the visitor cannot normally see, then the picture becomes clearer.

One of the subtleties of the Camargue is learning to discern which is a salt area and which is not.* Setting off in the north of the Camargue, having crossed the bridge from Arles and ventured into the delta, things look quite tame. The fields are a lush green in spring, and turn a rusty yellow, looking like burnt-out prairies in autumn. They are broken up by flourishing hedges and plenty of trees, and some points are almost high enough to look down over the ancient roofs of Arles. Everything looks fertile and the only bird life seems to be the unattractive greedy predators following in the wake of a tractor. For the higher Camargue is mainly agricultural land. At over three metres above sea level, it is salt-free and supports, very healthily, wheat, lucerne, fruits (particularly apples and tomatoes), vines, and Provençal cane. There are plenty of trees, as they survive in the salt-free earth, and they follow the ancient courses of the Rhône which once meandered across the emerging delta.

But, as the road goes southwards, so the vegetation begins to diminish. Lush greens give way to dry scrub land. Acres of scraggy grass and prickly bushes stretch before the eye, broken in places by desultory trees that appear to have a permanent stoop from the persistent force of the wind. Agriculture in its full variety has been supplanted by rice fields, monotonous in their regularity, though also exotic in appeal, with vast stretches of water reflecting visiting Egrets. Each paddy field (*rizière*) is divided by irrigation canals and in spring or autumn tractors can be seen sowing or harvesting, for the attractive sight of manual planting has now been taken over by huge machines. All that is now needed is the machine and two people standing at either end of the field holding a piece of string and a flag. Rice is difficult and temperamental to grow, but is the source of fierce local pride in *riz Camarguais* (which personally I find too soggy).

Still travelling south we come to the kind of landscape that

* I am indebted to a pamphlet by Luc Hoffman "An Ecological Sketch of the Camargue" (reprinted in *British Birds*, September 1958).

is the essence of the Camargue. This middle area, known as the *moyen Camargue*, is the beginning of what is perhaps the delta's biggest identifying feature: the *sansouire*. The *sansouire* means more than the French name for a salt-steppe; it's a name which obviously carries many other meanings to the locals. The salt-steppe is caked mud which supports the prickly-looking plant called *Salicornia*, or Glasswort, and the occasional, beautiful, filigree tree, the Tamarisk *Tamarix gallica*. The Tamarisks can withstand a certain amount of salt, but where salinity is highest and the trees have suffered from starvation conditions, beaten at the same time by the wind, the dried-out, dead-wood, skeletons of the past, can be seen fallen by the side of a salt lake, *étang*, or freshwater canal, *roubine*. In the upper *sansouire* of the middle Camargue, where the salinity is lower, the *Salicornia* is joined by the lovely mauve-flowered Sea Lavender, *Statice*, and by a kind of wild olive shrub, *Phyllyrea angustifolia*. It's also in the *sansouire* that you see the herds of Camargue bulls and the troops of Camargue horses. The horses are to be found around the edges of the marshes, for in the wild they feed on the reeds around freshwater marshes; the bulls feed, naturally, from the *Salicornia* and scrubby grasses. Only in the Camargue can such infertile ground be put to such good use. For a curious visitor, the saltiness of the earth can be tasted by licking a leaf of Glasswort.

There are both fresh and saltwater marshes in the Camargue, but it is the freshwater *marais* that have become most popularly known— the wide expanses covered with reeds and reedmace are well-known for their insalubrious setting. They are home too for the nesting Bitterns, Purple and Grey Herons and Water Rail. The Camargue was long feared for its unhealthy marshes and marsh fever, *fièvre paludéenne*, was the biggest deterrent to increased agricultural expansion for many a century. And, even today, if medicine can control the fever, nothing can control the stench and putrid atmosphere from the marshes. In their more open parts, they seem prettier; where the reeds have thinned out there are also Pondweed and Water Buttercups and hundreds of little marsh frogs as well as freshwater fish like

carp, rudd, catfish, pike and perch. For fisherman, though, the
happiest hunting grounds are the *roubines*, the canals bringing
irrigation water to the fields and paddies. In spring and summer
they are picturesquely lined with reeds and Yellow Flag, *Iris
pseudacorus*; in October with St John's Wort, *Hypericum perfora-
tum*, also yellow and wildly prolific.

Before we leave the middle Camargue, we have to stop by
one of the delta's most beautiful and original sights—the huge
expanse of water called the Étang de Vaccarès, which spreads
over sixteen thousand acres and merges interminably with the
sky. Vaccarès is haunting and mystical. It looks like the internal
sea it once was. Vaccarès is, in a way, the pivotal point of the
Camargue, controlling the balance of its waters. Local legends
say that Vaccarès is bottomless; it intrigues and is respected by
resident and visitor alike. But, even if it is not exactly bottomless
then it is certainly lower than sea level. It is connected with the
smaller *étangs* (known collectively as the *étangs inférieurs*) and
thereby controls the whole system.

In the past, any rain or flood water coming into the Camargue
was drained by a natural process into Vaccarès. Vaccarès does
not drain into the sea or into the river, so the water stays there.
Yet it has never become a stagnant or dying pool, for the water
was kept moving in two ways. The wind is the biggest factor;
particularly the powerful north-westerly, the *mistral*, which
blows water out of Vaccarès into the *étangs inférieurs* and into the
sea. This effect is countered by the south-easterly winds blowing
in from the coast carrying sea water into Vaccarès. The changing
levels on the great *étang* can look, on a chart, like ocean waves,
with as much as a metre's difference in the water level in the
north or south, depending on the direction of the wind. As the
*mistral* is the stronger wind and as the rivers kept flooding, a
lot of freshwater also found its way into Vaccarès. Another
element enters the picture: the hot, drying sun. In summer,
evaporation was the main method by which water left the
*étang*. In the old days some of the *étangs inférieurs* would dry up
completely, Vaccarès itself almost disappearing, making it
possible to walk across it. That kind of evaporation also allowed

the salt below the ground to work its way into the water, so the balance of salinity was maintained. That was why Vaccarès remained a saline lagoon, despite all the flooding; why the great *étang* was full of sea-water fish and was much loved as an internal sea. Now, though, something has changed.

Round the edge of Vaccarès have grown enormous clumps of reed; a clear and greatly feared sign to the ecologist that the massive input of freshwater for the rice fields has drastically altered the Camargue's natural balance. Vaccarès is becoming a freshwater lake, and now the variety of fish found there is decisive evidence. In itself, a freshwater lake is neither bad, nor boring, nor undesirable; but for Vaccarès, with its history and significance, it is. Ecologists have studied that kind of evolution over the past few decades, and to some degree it has already been kept under control. For the Camargue's vegetation is extremely vulnerable to changes in the environment.

Only Vaccarès, in the whole system, has no direct flow to the sea and is dependent on wind for its overflow movements. The smaller *étangs* (of the lower Camargue) are not in the same danger of losing their salinity as they are constantly refilled with sea water. It is to these *étangs*, and to the salty islets between them, that the wintering Ducks and Flamingoes come to find a resting place. In summer they are covered in huge floating masses of *Ruppia maritima* and the surfaces of the smaller pools are alive with yellow flowers. The land that breaks up these salty pools, the land that forms this lower part of the delta, is still *sansouire* but the salt-steppe supports much less *Salicornia* and is generally completely flooded in winter. Camargue bulls are still found grazing even at this point, and this is dangerous in winter when they can fall into a salt pool, as they are unable to judge its depth. From here, though, the Camargue slowly changes to the salt pans, *salins*, where saltwater is crystallised under the sun; and to the beach and the dunes. To the east and west of the Camargue, the dunes rise to nine metres in height and are actually among the most important dunes in the western Mediterranean, visited by botanists from all over the world. They extend for fifty kilometres and are covered in

Marram Grass, *Amphilia arenciria*, in May and June, but in summer they flower with Medick, Chamomile and Everlasting Flowers. But, it is the White Lilies growing on the highest points, and the spring Umbrella Pines, which are the most well-known and loved.

For most people the most fascinating part of the Camargue is that mysterious and now restricted area of ancient dunes, known as the Bois des Rièges. Just south of Vaccarès, in the middle of the area of *étangs* and parched *sansouire*, they form the strip of land that divides the great Vaccarès from the lesser *étangs*. A strange high point amid the flatness, they act as a barrier and there is a sense of mystery about them which has given rise to many legends.

These ancient dunes still stand on freshwater and are covered in trees, shrubs and some vegetation which is over four hundred years old. The Bois des Rièges is the haunt of Joseph D'Arbaud's mythical and symbolic beast in the story *La Bête du Vaccarès*, and the centre of many a local ghostly story. It is, in fact, the old coastline of the Camargue where, in centuries past, the delta finished before further centuries of the rivers' movements added to its acreage. The woods stand on freshwater because an ancient course of the Rhône once ran horizontally across the delta and formed the shore line. There are still seven *Bois*, on separate islets, covering eight kilometres and divided from each other by *sansouire* or, sometimes, perilous *gases* (uncharted stretches of water). They are now as lonely and deserted as anywhere in the Camargue; deserted mainly because they are part of the Réserve lands where entry is restricted. Even in the days when the dunes were grazing ground for the bulls, they had a prehistoric atmosphere. In the middle of the *Bois* you would be twenty kilometres from the northern farmhouses, and twelve kilometres from where the first car can be seen.

Today's visitors to the *Bois* tend to be botanists drawn by the virgin ground and rare finds; particularly by the growth of Phoenician Juniper trees which rise to a height of twenty metres (and that's high on a delta), and which are between three and four hundred years old. They are the only trees of their kind in

*Razeteurs* and Camargue bull at a *course libre* in the arena at Fontvieille

Patrick Castro, the *razeteur*, moves across the path of the bull

Little Egret feeding in a rice paddy in the Upper Camargue

Wild boar, *sangliers*, in the Bois des Rièges

Europe. The *Bois* are a kind of no-man's-land where the stillness and the sense of nature's dominance is overwhelming. As the casual visitor is not encouraged to visit this extraordinary part of the Camargue we shall join Eric Coulet, the young ecologist and scientific director of the Réserve Zoologique et Botanique de Camargue, who spends his days trekking out to the *Bois* studying the vegetation and bird life, insects and water creatures, for the control study he is making of the area. This way one can perceive some of the mysteries that belong less to the imagination than to nature's own system. He travels by boat or horse, as no car is allowed on to the Réserve lands. Occasionally parties of Camargue residents may be accompanied on horseback, for though they may have lived there a lifetime, they have been unable to visit the *Bois* since 1929.

To make the visit, Eric Coulet must start the day before the sun rises as, when it reaches its height, the *Bois* can be stifling, windless, and menacing with their prickly vegetation. Winter is a different prospect as most of the *sansouire* is under water or iced over. But once spring has come, the sun can burn and the mosquitoes attack. The Réserve has one of its guard's houses at Salin de Badon, on a horizontal line level with the *Bois*. The two guards who work there are in control of the eight Camargue horses belonging to the Réserve, which are not stabled, but roam free in the nearby pastures. For a day's ride, the horse first has to be lassoed and brought in, and then saddled. All of which takes time. Travel by horse, over the dry, mud-caked ground, and then over the stretches of water, is by far the easiest method, as the horse will never get lost. You could ride him without guiding, and he would take the quickest route back, avoiding bottomless drops in the *gases*. The only worry is the wild boar, *sangliers*, who live in the *Bois*, and who are so unused to any other presence that they can rush out and startle the horse. It was probably such an occasion that gave rise to D'Arbaud's darkly imaginative tale of the Beast of Vaccarès.

It takes two hours on horseback to the *Bois*, skirting round the Étang du Fournelet, past calmly feeding Flamingoes, over

C

dried up *sansouire* where the mud makes fish scale patterns, then
into the water wading over the *gases* of Cassieu and the infamous
Trou de Mon Oncle. Riders have been known to watch a friend
slowly disappearing as the horses's feet take him deeper and
deeper into the water, until the horse ends up swimming and the
rider gripping for his life. The stretches of water are sometimes
half a mile wide, the movement is slow and swishing, feet
dangling in the water and body moving to the animal's slow,
rhythmic, back-swaying gait. No fiery bad-tempered horses are
wanted for this kind of work as they delight in throwing the rider
into the water; but then the good-tempered ones have a habit of
deciding to go to sleep in the middle of the water or just stopping
and refusing to move. Alone under the sun and treading water
across the *gases*, a man has time to think. The horse rests after
about an hour as the flies, mosquitoes and *arabies* attack from
all quarters. Sometimes crossing the *gases* in mid-summer,
you can see a trail of blood pouring from the horses' insect
bites.

But as the journey progresses, it's the changing vegetation
that greets the eye. It gradually begins to shift from the
predominant sturdy *Salicornia* to a more exotic display of flowers,
narcissus, *Narcissus tazetta*, and *Asphodelus cerasifer* (the Asphodel
thought by the Greeks to be the flower of the dead which lined
the slopes of the underworld). They are found in several places
in the Camargue but nowhere so large, so brilliantly petalled
or so profuse as in the *Bois*. Here, approaching the *Bois*, is a
unique four-foot high Asphodel. There are Mediterranean
roses, such as Sage-leaved Cistus, *Cistus salvifolius*, and even Red
Poppies. But, overall, the air is dominated by the dry, musky
North African scent which rises from the inaptly named Stinking
Everlasting, *Helichrysum stoechus*, whose small yellow flower is
everywhere.

Kicking his way out of the last stretch of water and finding
his feet on the slippery banks, Badon the horse climbs into what
looks like a simple copse of trees suspended in the middle of a
vast desert. It is these unique thicket-forming trees of Phoenician
Juniper that makes the *Bois* look so unusual, though the dunes

are also densely covered with other shrubs such as the Mastic tree, *Pistacia lentiscus*, Mediterranean Buckthorn, *Rhamnus alaternesus*, and the creeper which lent its name to the *Bois*, *Phyllyrea angustifolia*, a wild olive shrub with prickly leaves known in Provençal as *l'arriège*. The shrubs are all spiky and heavily scented and beneath them are the platform beds of the wild boar, open yet quite secure in this haven of woods. The *Bois* is not really a place for sitting and dreaming. The mosquitoes and *arabies* are all over, sometimes covering whole arms and backs in thick swarms; the horse is uncomfortable as there is no water to drink and no shade and it's a two-hour walk back to the guard's house. So they leave, and the absolute quiet is disturbed temporarily by a gentle plodding, the swishing noise as the horse goes through the water, and a few birds wheel and cry overhead.

The Réserve lands are at the heart of the Camargue and contain most of what is really interesting to the naturalist. They include the Étang de Vaccarès, about one-third of the total area of the Réserve, the Bois des Rièges, the beautiful Étang du Fournelet and some of the land towards the Digue de la Mer. The Réserve Zoologique et Botanique de Camargue was formed in 1929 when the Camargue's natural ecological balance had begun to be noticed as something of value and it was then that the first steps were taken to arrest unwanted evolutionary developments. A step for which Camarguais have every reason to be thankful.

What had happened was that in 1854, in Paris, a society of naturalists called the Société Nationale d'Acclimatation de France had been formed. In 1928 the SNd'AF had the good fortune to be offered the management of a large area of the Camargue which was owned by the salt companies. Salt had always been "farmed" in the Camargue, even back to prehistoric days, and at this time the salt pans were owned by several companies such as Péchiney and the Salins d'Est. Their owners had bought up large tracts of unproductive land in the middle of the Camargue in an effort to protect themselves from

encroaching irrigation water from the Rhône. It wasn't so much
that the salt farmers were concerned for the ultimate fate of
Vaccarès or the Bois des Rièges, but rather that if the irrigation
processes were allowed to get too near to the salt pans, then the
production of sea salt would have been hampered. There was
another likely motive: the wealthy salt producers were also
keen hunters and it had not gone totally unnoticed that the
favourite sea birds for their sport loved the salty islets round the
pans—again the prospect of irrigation water desalinating the
coastal strip was not desired. In their favour (whatever the
reasons, they *were* ultimately saving the Camargue) is the fact
that the companies knew they had already altered the face of
the Camargue by their levelling and squaring operations in
forming the neat, geometrical shapes of the pans (*salins*), and
the feeling was that they wanted to offer the rest of the delta
some protection.

So, although the Réserve which was finally formed in 1929
had primarily been set up as a buffer zone between commercial
agriculture and commercial salt production, the land, once it
was handed over to the kind gentlemen in Paris, was indeed
cared for. The territory in the Camargue was the first piece of
land that the SNd'AF was able to protect. Strict rules in favour
of nature and to the disadvantage of humans were made, which
would be impossible today when, although there is more concern
that land should be protected, it is also felt that it should be
available for leisure purposes. It was ruled that entry would
be limited to naturalists and ornithologists and then only
with written permission from Paris. No one had the right to
take away one stick, flower or bird's feather (let alone eggs)
from the land; and there was to be no hunting, fishing or
trapping.

The salt companies had leased the land to the SNd'AF for
seventy-five years. But since then, after the Salins du Midi
parent company was formed in 1961 and the interest in conservation became world-wide and more urgent, the Camargue
was declared an area of conservation by the Council of Europe
in 1965, and the State, through the new Ministry of the

Teal over the Marais de St Serens

Flamingoes' nests in the Étang de Fangassier

Les Saintes-Maries-de-la-Mer, showing the Musée de Baroncelli-Javon

The tomb of Le Marquis Folco de Baroncelli-Javon at Le Simbéu

Environment formed in 1971, was able to come to an arrange-
ment with the Salins du Midi in 1972. They took over all the
Réserve lands for the nominal sum of one franc and bought
some more from the company. In return, the salt company was
allowed to transform more of the flat wastes by the sea into
salt pans. The Réserve territory is now forty square miles, the
extra land being about seven thousand five hundred acres. The
Ministry of the Environment still leaves the management of the
Réserve to the society in Paris which had become, in 1960, the
Société Nationale de Protection de la Nature et d'Acclimatation
de France—and so the Réserve was freed from worries over its
future.

The purchase of the new land for the Réserve, interestingly
enough, was made possible in 1971 by a gift to the State of five
million francs from the World Wildlife Fund, whose vice-
president is Luc Hoffmann of the Tour du Valat. Hoffmann
is one of the most significant men of the Camargue, whose rôle
in its future is inestimable. Hoffmann's family owns the wealthy
Swiss chemical and drug firm of Hoffmann-La Roche (he is
known locally as the King of Aspirin) and he first came to the
Camargue in 1947 as a student of zoology to do some field
studies. He was so impressed by the area that when in 1950 he
was back in the delta again and found he had the chance to buy
up a vacant *mas* and its forty thousand acres, he took on the
crumbling and decaying Tour du Valat and created the *station
biologique*. The *mas* is slightly off the beaten track and so
Hoffmann manages to keep some privacy and anonymity. The
house is attached to an old tower, one of the fortresses on an
ancient channel of the Rhône, and the farmstead includes a
farmhouse and stables, as well as a new laboratory, residential
quarters and even a schoolhouse for the employee's children.
But, more interesting to Hoffmann, the land he bought with
the *mas* includes most of the representative types offered in the
Camargue: some freshwater marsh in the *marais* de St Seren,
*sansouire* and agricultural land. His territory comes under as
much protection as does that of the Réserve. Hunting and
fishing are forbidden on or near the Tour du Valat. I'll come

to the kind of work Hoffmann and his assistants are engaged in later.

About one-third of the Camargue's land surface is protected in one way or another. The final Réserve area, known as Les Impériaux, is twelve square miles of *étang* and some *sansouire*, which lies to the north of Les-Saintes-Maries-de-la-Mer and was bought from the department Bouches-du-Rhône to protect the fishing industry for the local community. This Réserve is administered by the commune of Les-Saintes and while hunting is forbidden, fishing is merely restricted to those who earn a livelihood from the trade.

Finally, the Regional Park of the Camargue has to be mentioned. An administrative body whose intention is to co-ordinate all local interests for the greater protection of the delta, it does not actually own, or directly control, any land, and so is not a significant nature conserver.

Protected land or not, the visitor to the Camargue cannot help but be surprised that such so-called "wild" land is almost totally prohibited to the visitor. Coming along either of the roads south from Arles, some of the most striking features are perhaps the fencing and notices saying *défense d'entrer*. Apart from the Réserves and protected land, the Camargue is actually a mosaic of private properties, the land divided neatly up between the different owners. But, strangely, this is an important factor in the area's preservation. To the north of the Camargue most of the land is now put to agricultural use; to the south it has been left as it was with its marshes, scrub land and uncultivated parts, which presumably could have been drained and put to valuable use. Again, the motivating force was the Frenchman's love of hunting. One thing Camarguais knew instinctively was that its large and flourishing wild life, including the thousands of wild duck arriving every winter, were only coming because they were attracted to the natural habitat. And luckily, this proved to be an economical system. The majority of the *mas* and *domaines* to the south are also *réserve de chasse* which means two things: that the land brings in an economical return for the owner, and that the territory is left untouched. Even the

Réserve is prepared to compromise over hunting. Figures of bird populations have not yet decreased because of hunting and on the whole it seems a lesser evil than the despoliation of the whole of the Camargue for different economic returns. The delta is a nature reserve and a place where people live. The paradox is part of its character.

# Chapter 5

## THE LONG AND WINDING RHÔNE

For centuries the Camargue has known how to keep that stroppy little newcomer, man, in his place. There was a balance, an understanding, between *homo sapiens* and nature which allowed man to farm and exploit the land for his own uses, while he was at the mercy of nature's whims. She could raise a storm, flood the rivers' banks, carry the sea treacherously inland and reclaim its lost territory. And this is what happened. The saltiness of the earth made it largely unexploitable without river water irrigation and that was hardly possible when the whole area was under threat of being submerged by sea water.

For it was water that controlled the Camargue, formed as it was by century after century of the Rhône's downward slide to the sea. The great river had already left behind all its heavy material by the time it reached the flat land by the sea and could only deposit alluvial mud, sand and silt. What makes the Rhône's exit to the sea different from other rivers' is that it very quickly loses height, and at Lyons, one hundred and ninety-three miles up stream, its height is only five hundred and fifty-five feet; so for its last two hundred miles its fall is not more than two feet a mile. Then the prevailing winds of the Camargue completed the job; the north-westerly *mistral* and the equally forceful south-easterly made sure the sand and silt stayed where they were laid.

The average height of the Camargue is under a fifth of a metre above sea level, though it reaches a peak of height of between five and seven metres where the alluvial deposits were

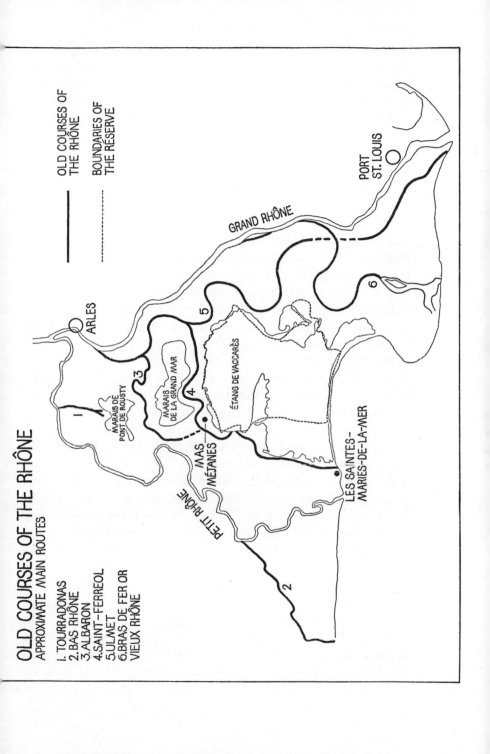

# OLD COURSES OF THE RHÔNE
APPROXIMATE MAIN ROUTES

1. TOURRADONAS
2. BAS RHÔNE
3. ALBARON
4. SAINT–FERREOL
5. ULMET
6. BRAS DE FER OR VIEUX RHÔNE

OLD COURSES OF THE RHÔNE

BOUNDARIES OF THE RÉSERVE

ARLES

GRAND RHÔNE

PORT ST. LOUIS

PETIT RHÔNE

MARAIS DE PONT DE ROUSTY

MARAIS DE LA GRAND MAR

MAS MÉJANES

ÉTANG DE VACCARÈS

LES SAINTES–MARIES-DE-LA-MER

built up on either side of the river's courses. The Camargue's history follows, quite literally, the courses of the Rhône. As the various tributaries meandered their way across the delta, alluvial deposits built up in the river's bed, until finally the water itself was forced out. The river would change its course leaving in its wake fertile agricultural land on its immediate banks, and marshes where the old course had run.

The first settlements grew up along those ancient courses; farmhouses, towers and fortresses were built along the old banks for protection from river invasions and for optimum use of the fertile land. In some of the *mas*, old wells can be found that went down to the bed of the river and still provide fresh water supplies. As the Camarguais themselves say, the history of their land is inextricably tied to the movements of the river, where it had run and what it left beside it.

But even more interesting, the Camargue of today is about one-third larger than when it first entered the chronicles of history at the time of the first Greek occupation. This is where some digging around in the local library, the Bibliothèque Nationale in Arles, unearths as yet uncollected information. It is believed, for instance, that the limits of the Camargue in the Greek era (around the sixth century BC), were to be found along one of the ancient courses of the Rhône which ran in a horizontal line from the present towns of Grau-du-Roi to Fos-sur-Mer (and which is also the line formed by the ancient dunes of the Bois des Rièges). As the Provençal historian and archaeologist, Jean-Paul Clébert, has found, one can see exact raised traces, using ancient maps of the library in the Borely museum at Marseilles, representing the Provençal Marseilles of earlier times. The ancient river bank, he claims, was cut into by various smaller river mouths (called *grau* in Provence) and some ports like the original Roque d'Odor and Les-Saintes.

Before the Greeks raided the Ligurian coast, as the south of France was then known, the Camargue's marshes and islands already had a place in Greek mythology as being similar in lay-out to the Hydrus of Lerna. The Étang de Vaccarès and smaller *étangs* behind the Rhône, as I have said, did form an enclosed sea at the centre of the delta, but in those days the land was higher and heavily forested above that line.

The disappearance of the forests of the Camargue is one of the delta's unsolved mysteries. There are many theories put forward to explain why it now bears only a few trees. One theory is based on the idea that the old coastline once had a number of flourishing ports which are now untraceable. The theory is that there was a considerable drop in the height of the land which led to the area being denuded of its vegetation. This theory was explored by Oldham, an English geologist of the 1930s who had studied the Camargue, by comparing writings from the archives. He quotes a local engineer, Denizet, who had guessed that various depressions in the land surface could explain the disappearance of the buildings in the Roman ports. For none of the docks, warehouses and public buildings remain for our scrutiny.

Oldham then collated evidence that substantiated this theory. He wrote that the original alluvial deposits of the delta were, by Roman times, sufficiently high to be beyond further silting up and it was on this land that they built their houses. In Roman times, the mouth of the Rhône would have lain sixteen Roman miles from the port of Fossae Maritimae (now Fos-sur-Mer), across to Grau-de-la-Dent at the mouth of what we now call the Vieux Rhône. But, by the twelfth century, Fossae as a sea-port had totally disappeared. There was only one solution, he says: a general subsidence in the country and a submergence of the lower levels of the delta. He dates this, more precisely, by saying that at the beginning of the eighth century, the port of Fossae was still as important as it had been in Roman times. From the middle of the ninth century, Fossae was superseded by Arles as a port. The subsidence, he concludes, must have taken place between the beginning of the eighth and the end of the ninth centuries. He then compares this with evidence of an earlier subsidence. In *Ore Maritimae*, the Greek chronicler Festus Avienus describes the course of the Rhône, from its source, and says that before reaching the sea, it enters a great marsh known as Accion and then branches west. This Lake Accion had been silted up even by Roman times and has now disappeared. It has been identified, though, as the old marsh to the east of Belle-garde, which was swallowed up in the construction of the canal from Aigues-Mortes to Beaucaire.

From this evidence Oldham concluded that there had been two land falls, which were rapid and perhaps traumatic for the region. Other theories about the disappearance of the forests of the Camargue, connected with man's presence in the delta, will appear in the next chapter.

Meanwhile, however, the old battle between the sea and the river raged on, the one leaving its deposits and the other washing them away, constantly changing the beds of the Rhône. These ancient courses have been traced, though only at such time as they finished, giving place to a new course, because the archives record not so much the changing river patterns, as the effects of terrible flooding or storms in which somebody either lost sheep or cattle, or where fights may have ensued over the consequent ownership of land. The dating of these ancient courses is not exact, and tends to be spoken of in terms of centuries, but placing them is important to an understanding of the present structure of the delta (see map on page 73).

The oldest known tributary, the Tourradonas, the one which led to Lake Accion, changed course around the tenth century; this was a relatively small river in the far north of the delta. In the twelfth century, the course known as the Bas-Rhône finished. It had run to the west of the present-day Petit Rhône leaving in its wake the *étangs* de Gines, Consecanière and Launes and the *marais* du Couvin. A major branch of the Rhône used by the Romans, as a route from Arles to Albaron, ran well to the north of Vaccarès just below the *mas* du Pont du Rousty. It was known as Albaron and came to an end in the thirteenth century. One of the most important was the Saint-Ferréol river which finally ran out in the fourteenth century and cut across directly to the north of Vaccarès below the Grand Mar, the huge *marais* in the middle of the Camargue, and then flowed down the side of the great *étang* where large *mas* such as Méjanes were constructed on its banks. Ulmet was the principal river leading from Arles into the sea at Port St Louis; it was used by the Romans as a means of transport and its meandering route was presumably the reason for their measurement of thirty miles from Arles to the sea. Ulmet disappeared in the Middle Ages. The course known as Sylvéréal finished in the sixteenth century and ran on the edge of the Petite Camargue; Bras Mort, on the right bank of the Grand Rhône, also ran out in the sixteenth century and finally, the famous Bras de Fer, known today as the Vieux Rhône, came to an end in the eighteenth century, when the Rhône was first embanked in its two present courses, and is still used as a major irrigation canal, the Canal de Japon.

Many of the irrigation canals which now thread their way round the Camargue, bringing fresh water from the Rhône, have picked up the courses of the old tributaries of the great river, especially in the north from the Saint-Ferréol. For centuries the Camarguais wanted to control and understand their rivers, but the final geomorphological map work was not done until between 1967–70 when the company responsible for the extensive drainage scheme in the marshes of Languedoc-Roussillon, undertook an intensive survey of the Camargue, tracing the old courses, and printing the definitive map (on which the map on page 73 is based) of alluvial deposits and salt content. The work runs to twenty volumes and is regarded by Camargue farmers as their bible.

But the most important date in the history of the Camargue is that of the embanking of the Rhône—man's first step to control the natural balance and water system. Most people put the date at between 1711 and 1720, which was when the river was first trained into its two present courses, Grand and Petit. But this early embankment, using simply dug out channels and wooden supports, was still not strong enough to withstand all the rigours of a Camargue winter. The land continued to be flooded by the sea, and to be affected by subterranean salt, while not being flooded in the same measure by the rivers, which meant the salt concentration in the soil increased drastically.

For a whole century and more, the process of change was slow. Man's presence in the delta was not felt till the year following the great storms and floods of 1856 when the sea came twenty kilometres inland, drowning whole herds of bulls. In 1857–8, the State built a dyke across the sea front. The new dyke, the Digue de la Mer, is a barrier just over two metres high and forty-five kilometres long. Alongside it old wooden poles of earlier dykes are still standing in the water: wood is the only material that is not corroded by salt. At the same time the local civic engineers finally embanked the two branches of the Rhône. Now the Camargue could no longer be submerged by either sea or river and man had played his biggest trump card against nature. Surely there was nothing to stop him taking control? But the next thing we hear is that by the 1930s scientists were getting very worried that the Camargue was drying up. The level of Vaccarès was very low and there was even talk that now was the time to drain it completely and free the land for agriculture. Instead, a system of irrigation canals and pumping stations from the Rhône was introduced. There was no particular motivation at the time for intensive drainage schemes. The world didn't need so much food then. But things changed. The problem of Vaccarès drying up was soon to become a short-lived nightmare.

## Chapter 6

## "THE PROCESS OF MAN'S OCCUPATION OF THE DELTA WAS THE SAME AS MAN ALWAYS TAKES . . ."*

IT WAS MANY centuries before man learned to exploit nature and put pressure on the delta. The history of mankind in the delta is not too easy a story to follow as it is surprisingly sparsely documented. Papers are still being discovered and new information revealed. There have been many excellent historians, archaeologists and archivists in the area: from Quiqueran de Beaujeu in the sixteenth century, to Fernand Benoit, the early twentieth-century archivist from Arles, and Jean-Paul Clébert, the contemporary Provençal historian and archaeologist. Yet inhabitants of the Camargue, recently awakened to a new sensibility about their land, even now swap papers and documents and try to fit together the pieces of the pattern of their past. They can speak of the three important stages they know about: the Greek traders who first settled in the Camargue; the Roman legionaries who built their wealthy villas there, and the famous monks from the "abbeys of salt", the religious orders of the Middle Ages who became rich from the sale of salt. It's a rich and colourful history, though peppered with doubt and conflicting opinions.

If the delta is sometimes described as a vast primeval landscape then at least we know that prehistoric man was there to

* "Le processus de l'occupation du delta est identique à celui que l'on constate chaque fois que l'homme à pris pied dans une région inhabitée." From the first publication of the Parc Naturel Régional de Camargue, January 1973, issued to introduce the Camargue to visitors.

enjoy it. Archaeological remains are hard to come by in a marshy district, under water for half the year, but some bones have been discovered supporting the theory that the descendants of Bronze Age man—tribes known as the Ligurians— would have either lived in, or used, the Camargue. They may have come down from the hills of Provence fleeing from attacks from other tribes, and entered the dubious sanctuary of this unwelcoming area, which then would have been densely forested and criss-crossed with odd tributaries of the Rhône— but also offering rich treasure in the shape of the wild birds, the fish and the fruits on the trees.

The first recorded history of the Camargue tells of the arrival of the Greeks around 650 BC. They came from Rhodes and settled along the Rhône between Arles and the sea. Then, and it's not known why two separate waves of exploration should have occurred, around 600 BC another batch arrived from Phocea and settled along the Mediterranean coast. These later Greeks from the northernmost Ionian cities on the west coast of Asia Minor were not warlike people, but were more like business men. The Ligurian coast was already known to them through national legends: the mouth of the great river Rhône was sometimes depicted as the gateway to hell. But, being wise business men, they ignored the mythology and the mouth of the Rhône proved hospitable. They had to apply to the Ligurian king Namnos, seated in what was actually to become Arles and which was then called Théliné, for permission to set up trading stations at the mouth of the Rhône; the river was then running in the horizontal line between Grau-du-Roi and Port-St Louis. It was this trading station, set up near the mouth, that was the birth and beginnings of Massillia—later, of course, to grow into Marseilles. They set up other posts and stations along the coast of the delta, the mysterious disappearing towns referred to in the previous chapter. The only surviving ports originally set up by the Phoceans are Les-Saintes (then much further inland) and Fos-sur-Mer.

As their energies were directed towards trade, rather than territorial expansion, the Ligurian and Phocean populations co-existed in harmony. Later, even the generally warlike Celtic tribes from the north, who envied them the valley of the Rhône, managed to live peacefully with this mixed population. The port of Massillia flourished and the people enjoyed wealth and some of the decadence that seems to accompany successful trading. The Greeks became firmly rooted in this southern area of France and played an important part in its singular history. The area is still referred to as Rhodanien; the Rhône itself as the *voie rhodanien*, or, by its Greek name Rhodanos.

But it was the Roman presence that had the most long-lasting effect on southern France and on the Camargue. The name of Provence, of course, meant Roman province; but it remained as a separate state, only becoming a part of France in the fifteenth century. The Romans first came to France to protect the Ligurians from the increasingly warlike Celtic tribes to the north. The Ligurians had previously helped Rome by sending men and money to them when Hannibal marched from Spain, across the Rhône and into the Alps, threatening Italy with his sixty thousand infantry, nine thousand cavalry and his elephants. When the Ligurians in turn appealed to Rome for help in 128 BC, Caius Sextus Calvinus marched into southern France, defeated the Celts and founded present-day Aix-en-Provence. It was another Roman general, though, who became the much adored hero for saving the Ligurians from Barbarian raids across the Alpilles. Caius Marius stood his ground against the Barbarians, wiping them out in 102 BC. It was he whose name is supposedly the root of the name of the Camargue. But, again, there are many opposing theories.

Michel Droit, a local writer and historian, has laid down the three basic choices for the history of the delta's name. One, that the name signifies the existence of an ancient medieval divinity called Camars. Two, that it comes from the Celto-Ligurian word, *ca-mar*, meaning land reclaimed from the water and used in Languedoc expressions like *cara-marca* (beloved frontier), or *n'a cap marca* (has no frontier). Three, and a popular theory, is that it honours the memory of Caius Marius, as in *Caii Marii ager*, meaning the fields of Caius Marius. There is another theory, chosen by some, that the name derives from Aulus Annius Camars, a Roman country gentleman who owned a large estate called *L'Insula Camarica*. It was he who first raided the herds of wild Camargue horses and put them to use in the games in the arena.

Before the Roman presence, the Greeks were already well settled in Théliné, present-day Arles, which even then faced the port of Trinquetaille across the river, known as Rhodanusia. It was not until 49 BC, when Julius Caesar took Massillia (Marseilles) and arranged to have twenty warships built in Arles, that the town began to achieve any status or size. Julius Caesar founded a colony at Arles and in 46 BC sent six thousand war veterans of the Sixth Legion to settle there—it became known as Arelate or Sextanorum Colonia Arelas. Greek residents and the new Roman inhabitants worked together putting up the arena, theatre, stadium, baths and the usual accoutrements of Roman living. It has been said that they were built with Greek robustness and Roman grace. Arles began to rival Massillia and became known as "the little Rome of Gaul". The Legionaries, being wealthy and used to the good life, took up residence in the Camargue where they built villas and villages on the higher ground. The Camargue became home to a prosperous class; a memory of wealth the delta was not to forget, though there were years of poverty and misery before the contemporary families settled there. The Romans built roads linking Albaron, Villeneuve and Ulmet and used the Rhône for trade, transporting wood, resin, salt, brine and fish from coast to hinterland, and stone from hinterland to delta, to build their villas, as every piece had to be imported.

Yet not one Roman stone is now to be found: another of the mysteries of which the Camargue is proud. There are pieces of Roman pottery and coins, evidence enough of a civilisation, which crop up on higher ground and on the banks of Vaccarès, but there is no sign of homes or villas. The reason is simple enough. The delta, made up of alluvial silt, does not carry any pebbles. (To the east of the Camargue the area known as La Crau is all pebbles; the story goes that Hercules was going to cross the Crau but had been warned of ambushes from the Ligurians, and to help him Zeus covered the sky with clouds and made rain of stones in hail.) The Romans would have shipped in the stone from a place like Beaucaire, and in later centuries, when other Camarguais wanted to build homes, they might have used the relics to build their *mas*. A pile of archaic rubble is more use for rebuilding than as an historic monument. Then, of course, there is the argument about successive land height changes, the flooding by sea and river, and the consequent loss of buildings to the water. But that isn't the only mystery left by the Romans.

One of the most popular legends of the Camargue is that it reached a peak of economic prosperity under the Romans, when it was exploited as a granary for the growing town of Arles and for all the people of Provence. Where better, given the lack of interest in marshy lands, to cover the ground with wheat and oat crops? Caesar himself wrote in his Commentaries that the Camargue was a granary for the Gaul armies (*le grenier à blé de l'armée des Gaules*), which if true could expose the Romans as the ones who deforested the delta for their own uses. There is another theory which blames the Romans for denuding the region of its trees, claiming that they used the wood to build Caesar's ships, but that is open to question as the white wood of the area is not suitable for ship building. But how true is the granary story? Was the delta higher then and thus more easily used for agriculture?—for future generations certainly found crops such as wheat very hard to grow. The most northerly parts, near Arles, may have been used, but there is no evidence that the Romans were involved in massive drainage and land reclamation. The historian Jean-Paul Clébert disagrees with this theory, although he stands alone in this and spoils a nice tale. He holds that after the Roman period, during the Middle Ages, the Camargue was depopulated and exposed to the ravages of pirates. When peace finally returned, some landowners came back to pick up the pieces and what they found was a land of flourishing natural growth; prolific in wild game, animals and fish. Only a densely forested area, says Clébert,

could have led the contemporary chronicler Quiqueran de
Beaujeu to write of the surprising fertility of this country, the
excellence and variety of its produce.

In fact, it might have been the monks who started the drainage systems and chopped down the trees to build dykes and
homes. For the Camargue's next invaders were a hundred and
fifty peasant monks who founded and built the notable "abbeys
of salt" during the twelfth century. In 1157, the monks of
Bonnevaux founded the Abbey of Ulmet, whose ruins are still
there though hidden from sight on the Réserve lands. In 1200,
they moved to Sylvéréal to another abbey, founded by King
Alphonse of Aragon. There were also abbeys at Trinité,
Psalmodi and L'Abadié: all of them built along the old branch
of the Rhône that ran by the coastline. The monks made a good
living from the salt, known as the "white gold" of Provence.
But they were actually the first protectors of the Camargue;
ruling that no one was to destroy the trees on the land for
commercial use. The only tree cutting was to be for heating or
building of peasants' homes. The monks also provided sanctuary
and hospital care for the wounded soldiers returning from the
Crusades. Aigues-Mortes, the ancient fortified town to the west
of the Camargue, was used by the Crusaders as an embarkation
point and it has been pointed out that not only did the soldiers
come to the Camargue for their hospital care, and quarantine,
but for their burial ground too. The historian Fernard Benoit
wrote ghoulishly, that they were "quarantined in a deserted
area which was peopled with their bones".

For the rest, the history of the Camargue was inextricably
linked with the fate of Arles and of Provence. Glamorous and
wealthy Arles became the home of emperors and rulers. Its
arena had been built in the first century BC for twenty-one
thousand spectators and the amphitheatre for seven thousand.
It had an imperial mint, was the centre for the cloth industry
and the export centre for wine and oil. Emperor Honorius
(AD 418), who held a convention of all the representatives of
Gaul in Arles, once wrote, "It is from Arles that all the products
of the entire world are distributed: the Oriental luxuries, the

perfume of Arabia, the delicate products of Assyrian art, the grain of Africa, the fruits of Spain, and all the wealth of Gaul, are literally unloaded at this point".

But its history began to degenerate through a series of wars and between AD 465–869, Arles was besieged ten times, and pillaged seven times, by a series of invaders, all of whom left their mark on the Arlesian racial characteristics. These visitors included Visigoths, Franks, Ostrogoths and Saracens and not much of the splendour that was "the little Rome of Gaul" was left to plunder. Provence left the peaceful era of the Pax Romana and was ceded to the Franks. It was ruled by a succession of Frankish kings who delegated their power to representatives, *Patrices*, who took the opportunity of making Provence an independent state. They allied Provence with the Saracens and from 732, when the Saracens first laid siege on Arles, for the next three hundred years, the town was under their repressive rule. There is even now a strong Moorish influence in Arles; the Arlesian women, often fêted for their mysterious beauty (as in the paintings of Léo Lélé in the Muséon Arlaten), reputedly share the heavy features and dark hair of both their Greek and Moorish forefathers. But, at the beginning of the twelfth century, Arles was won back to the Holy Roman Emperor and Provence was divided into three subprovinces, governed by eighteen successive Counts, of whom René, ex-king of Naples, Charles III, Count of Maine, and Louis XI, King of France, were the last. Provence was finally united with the rest of France in 1487 by Charles VIII, and so ended one of the longest and earliest civilisations of the western world. It was a history of separatism which Provence was never to forget and is still found in the Provençal language, most notably, of course, used in the Camargue.

The Middle Ages were genuine dark ages for Provence and the arena at Arles was used to house the depleted population who sought protection from invasion and disease in the hastily constructed houses within its walls. The physical split between the patriarchal town of Arles and the rougher working sea-port of Trinquetaille grew, so that Trinquetaille was used as the receiving station for plague victims from Arles. Meanwhile, the Camargue reverted to a virtual desert. Its coast was plagued by pirate raids and several towers were built at the Rhône's mouths and up the river banks to protect them. The story of piracy in the Camargue is only now coming to light from the evidence of old papers. It seems that the area was regarded as a lost cause. It was outside civilian rule and was guarded instead by the army. To this day, it has retained a reputation for being a sanctuary for escaped prisoners. Farming continued there on a subsistence level, though the area was always used lucratively for hunting the wild birds and animals. The marshes were infested with fever and land exploitation was the last thing on anyone's mind. In the sixteenth century, records show that some formidable towers and look-out posts were built: the Tour d'Amphoux and the Tour de la Rougnouse. In the seventeenth century, the Tour de Tourvieille which is still, in part, standing, was put up to "inspect the boats going up and down the Rhône". Even the large private dwellings of the time were built as fortified châteaux. One such is the Château d'Albaron which protected the entrance to the Camargue on the Petit Rhône, and another is the beautiful Château de l'Armellière built by a business man of Arles in 1606 and still inhabited and privately owned—perhaps the oldest building still standing. The rest of the population lived in reed huts, the *cabanes*, which have now become the homes of the *gardians* or have been copied as holiday houses.

The few people who lived in the Camargue in the sixteenth century, did not live the ordinary French village life. There were no tradesmen or priests and life was very rough. One Lantelme de Romieu wrote in 1574 of the plagues of the Camargue which, considering the extent of the marshes, must have been terrifying. The Archbishop of Arles, Jean Jaubert de Barrault, who wanted to set up parishes in the delta because of the bleak picture he saw there, came down very heavily:

There are intolerable winds there. The island has a kind of heat that leads to despair, four or five months of the year.

There are gnats, and more, for two or three weeks in the summer there are flies (in Provençal called *arabies*) in their thousands of millions which lead to desperation. They bite all the time. . . . In most of the small farms there isn't a courtyard. The house is in the middle of the fields; one is completely open there, thirty times worse off than what you can see in Picardy or Marle. You find there people who have seen neither priest nor clergymen since they were ten or twelve years old, no mass and no confessions. (1635)*

The peasant farmers no doubt continued to eke out an existence guarding and rounding up the wild bulls and horses and selling some of the meat to the bourgeoisie of Arles. Fishermen would always have made a living in the village of Les-Saintes-Maries-de-la-Mer. But it was not an enviable situation.

By the seventeenth and eighteenth centuries, the Camargue saw a steady rise in fortunes. It is from this period that the large *mas*, seen there today, began to be constructed, and the land itself was put to use for more intensive agriculture. It was from 1711, when the Rhône was first embanked, that the beginning of irrigation of the salty earth with fresh river water can be dated. Some of the larger *mas*, like the Mas de Juge, de Vers, la Trésorière, Fiélouse, and the Châteaux de Giraud, de Méjanes and Armellière, became influential homes in the area. There were around two hundred *mas* by the eighteenth century and the ground turned out to be quite fertile for wheat and oats. The southern part, still a paradise for hunters, was used by a different kind of big property owner and the task of stock-breeding began to be taken seriously.

Yet until the nineteenth century, the Camargue remained a desolate, strange and much feared place. (An early attempt to grow rice which was permitted officially by Louis XV on 1st January 1741 was stopped by a royal *arrêt* in December 1747 because the danger of *fièvre paludéenne* was too great.) In 1806, an Arlesian businessman, Pierre Véran, described how Les-Saintes-Maries-de-la-Mer had been despoiled by the barbarians

* Quoted in *La Camargue* by Fernand Benoit.

who lived there, the church made into a house and the battlements sold off stone by stone. This was the image of the
Camarguais, rude and criminal by nature, which persisted and
perhaps, in some ways, still persists:

> The outskirts of the little town are not shaded by a single
> tree. One sees there not one garden. Vast cesspools out of
> which come the ceaseless odour of pestilential vapour make
> staying here quite intolerable and even those who live here
> often fall victim to the diseases. . . . Their character is gross
> and brutal; their manners, since the Revolution, are very
> bad. . . . No kind of industry, except for fishing and hunting.
> Like pirates, they are never as happy as when the sea is in
> turmoil and then, they climb to the top of their church, look
> out to sea and try to spot some building close to being
> submerged, and if that misfortune happens, you can see them
> running in the early morning, along the coast to gather up
> the booty from those who have perished during the tempest.*

In many ways, it has been this very lack of civilisation that
has attracted people to the Camargue. There are, of course, the
gypsies who come in May and October every year, for the
religious pilgrimage of the three Marys of Les-Saintes-Maries,
a festival which they have adopted to their own spiritual needs.
Somewhere the wild spirit of the gypsies identified itself with
the fighting spirit of the Camarguais. And, paradoxically, at
the end of the nineteenth century, came the Provençal renaissance, inspired by Frédéric Mistral, when the Camargue was
not only reassessed, but was seized upon as the ideal rustic and
rigorous background for man to feel his place in nature. All
that belongs to the story of Mistral, and his formidable disciple
le Marquis de Baroncelli-Javon, which I'll come to later.

Several of the families who live in the Camargue now, either
as farmers or stockbreeders, trace their ancestors back to the
early or middle nineteenth century. It is not a history that
reaches into the past; the Camargue has seen too many changes

* *Ibid.*

for that. But for a long time it mystified me. Why the gap? What happened to those people who lived there in earlier centuries? I think now it is answered by the mere brutality of the way of life. Families did not live and breed there; homes were not passed down from generation to generation. Human life was wild and untamed; just a few peasants, the odd pirate, fisherman and maybe an ex-convict, living in isolation in time and place. From the nineteenth century, the families began to build up their farms, and started stockbreeding. The wild bulls and horses of the delta were organised among the *manades*. Farming became an easier prospect and the way of life, that continues today, was established.

## Chapter 7

## A STORY OF SAINTS AND GYPSIES

---

SOMETIMES IT IS hard to imagine that Saintes (as Les-Saintes-Maries-de-la-Mer is known locally) is the legendary home of the first Christian community: but the legend of the Holy Marys of Saintes dates back before history into mythology and is one of the most fascinating of its kind. The history of the Camargue can never be told by repeating facts and figures, for more than half of it rests in mythology. The Provençaux, as a race, love to tell stories and, equally, love to believe them. Yet, sometimes, these strange tales seem incongruous in this thriving twentieth-century community. Saintes, for instance, is now a major tourist centre. Originally a little fishing village, it has attracted tourists for many years as the pilgrimage centre for both Christians and gypsies. But Saintes's real boom came with the advent of the two-week holiday, and the weekend sun-soak, bringing thousands from industrialised Marseilles, Nîmes and Avignon to its free beaches and hot summers. No more than St Tropez, is Saintes still a tiny, unspoilt, fishing village: which is somewhat surprising as the mosquitoes respect the tourist no more than the farmer, and though the town can look attractive on a sunny day, it can look fairly indifferent during the *mistral* and positively mean during the off-season.

Watching the gypsy festival, a free-for-all for camera-happy tourists in search of sensation, of hippies in search of freedom, and of gypsies in search of their friends, it is indeed hard to imagine Saintes as the home of western Christianity. Every roof is littered with human shapes as people fight for the best viewing places. Even the town's two public lavatories are adorned with bodies as is the sad figure of Christ on the crucifix, humiliated even further by camera-fanatics astride his out-stretched arms.

The legend of the Marys, again an amalgam of conflicting stories, says that after the Crucifixion, Mary Magdalene, Mary Jacobé, Mary Salomé, and Martha, together with their serving girl Sara, and with Lazarus, Maximim and Sidoine, were all chased out of Palestine and escaped in a small boat without oars or sails. The boat drifted at sea and finally came to rest on the coast of the Camargue where the Greek fortress of Oppidum Râ was standing. (*Râ* became adopted into Camarguais as *râtis*, meaning boat, and *radeau*, meaning a small islet in the middle of a lagoon, and perhaps even *Rièges* the name of the forest.)

The Marys were so grateful for their deliverance that they built their first primitive chapel in the fortress. Mary Jacobé, Mary Salomé and Sara stayed in the Camargue, founding the first Christian community there and were believed to have built a simple altar by hand. Lazarus took the Word to Marseilles, Maximim and Sidoine to Aix-en-Provence, while Mary Magdalene set off towards La Sainte-Baume but was led by angels into a grotto where she stayed, meditating and fasting, for thirty-five years. It was said that anyone approaching the grotto was liable to have his or her legs turned into lead. Meanwhile, Martha had had the most adventurous time. She went north to Tarasçon to combat the dragon—that had been menacing the local virgins, no doubt! The dragon, who lived in a lair on the bottom of the Rhône, would emerge from time to time to eat the good people. Martha tamed him and led him meekly through the streets, whereupon the good people stoned him to death. So, the forces of Christianity versus paganism were canonised again, being translated here, as everywhere, into fiery myth and legend.

The story differs sometimes: another version has it that it was the Virgin Mary herself who came in the boat, with Mary Magdalene and Sara. They set sail for Provence which was where Joseph of Arimathea had traded in tin. While at sea

Sara jumped overboard in fear but the angels took over the
situation so that when a cloak was thrown out to her, they
changed it into a raft, on which Sara sailed to safety.

Sara, however she may have arrived, is the saint adopted by
the gypsies of western and parts of eastern Europe. Hers is a
difficult story to trace. It may be that she was taken up by the
gypsies because she was a dark-skinned Egyptian girl and they
recognised one of their own kind. But another story goes that a
tribe of gypsies was already on the Mediterranean coast when
the Marys landed and that, led by one called Sara, they were
good to the Marys. Gypsiologists have pointed out that Saint
Sara is very similar to Sara le Kâli, the Indian goddess.
Contemporary theory has it that all gypsies date back to a
common home in India and their great dispersal has not
affected the fact that their language and customs come from
Indian culture. The dark-skinned Sara, serving girl to the
Marys, would have been taken up as their saint because she
reminded them of Sara le Kâli.

The first church, the one built by the Marys, was destroyed
by the Saracens in the ninth century. And thereby hangs
another legend. The Saracens, having outwitted the Arlesians,
managed to capture the Archbishop of Arles and hold him
for ransom at Saintes. The poor Archbishop died of natural
causes, while being held, but the Saracens covered up their loss,
stuffed him and stood him outside the church under a canopy.
The Archbishop appeared to be wrapped in godly meditation
and the Saracens had the last laugh when they came away with
the money. The church, which was built towards the end of the
twelfth century, still stands with its Moorish battlements intact.

For a long while the village was known as Notre-Dame-de-
Ratis, but later it became Notre-Dame-de-la-Mer and not until
1838 did it become Les-Saintes-Maries-de-la-Mer. It was put
on the secular map in 1448, by "good King René", then Count
of Provence, who dreamed up the idea of digging for the relics
of the Holy Marys, a plot hatched with the help of a papal
legate. They dug beneath the church, where it was believed the
Marys had built their altar and had been buried. They

The pilgrimage of the Marys

Pilgrims in the sea watching the saints being dipped into the water

A Camargue horse feeding from a salty *étang* near Les Saintes-Maries

unearthed, they said, a column, an ancient altar and actual relics of the saintly bones. René granted the town the privilege of becoming a pilgrimage centre which was, incidentally, also good for trade. The relics and the pilgrimage were sanctified by the Bishop of Marseilles on 7th January 1449, and the dates were fixed for 24th May, the saint's day of Mary Jacobé, and 22nd October, the day of Mary Salomé and for the first Sunday in December as the anniversary of the discovery of the relics. This Feast of the Revelation is a purely local ceremony.

The French Revolution was the only thing that stood in the way of the pilgrimages' popularity. On 5th March 1794 the church was sacked and the relics assumed burned but, by a typically Provençalian miracle, a curé had already smuggled them out and buried them, and returned them three years later.

The ceremony of 24th May has been growing in popularity every year, shared as it is by Christians and gypsies. The effigy of Sara did not join the Marys, however, until 1935 but now, since the gypsies outnumber the pilgrims, the two ceremonies take place side by side. Each of the saints has a small doll-like plaster body, painted in blues and pinks. For days before the ceremony, pilgrims and gypsies pour into the crypt of the church at Saintes, lighting candles, leaving clothes for the saints and praying for miracles to cure the sick and injured. In the crypt cards are pinned to the walls showing injured people's photographs and there are messages of thanks for help received. But on the morning of the 24th, the crowds who gather outside the church may be touched for contributions by those gypsies who come for the pickings rather than the worship. There is a service inside the church and then the famous lowering of the effigies down through a vault in the ceiling of the crypt. The two Marys are standing in their little boat and a banner to Sara, le Kâli, is carried separately.

Outside the church a throng of observers and photographers waits amid the stamping feet of the horses ridden by the leading *manadiers, gardians* and *chevaliers de Camargue*, splendid in their traditional clothes, ready to lead the procession off through the streets. The horsemen lead the way, *tridents* over their shoulders, and the crowd follows behind carrying the figures of the Marys and the banner to Sara. The Christians chant "Vive les Saintes Maries" and the gypsies echo "Vive la Sainte Sara". The crowd straddles the two narrow main streets, down to the coast road to the sea where, as a sudden silence descends, the statues are dipped into the sea in time-honoured style.

What the procession does for the religious few is questionable. For the town it attracts some eighty thousand people in one long weekend, including eight thousand gypsies in trailers and caravans, the usual French anti-nomad rules being generously lifted for those few days. The town is alive with flamenco, and groups of young boys and girls stroll the streets, loving the sound of the music, clapping their hands and breaking into dance. It's an occasion for drinking, dancing and fun—for all. By the end of the night there might be a few fights as the townspeople forget their gains and suddenly become annoyed at the intrusion of their privacy.

But most unforgettable, is the sight of the gypsies who have gathered from nearby centres such as Sète or Marseilles; or who have come not only from England, Holland, Scandinavia, Germany and of course Spain, but also from Czechoslovakia, Poland and Hungary. Their caravans, ranging from the most luxurious to the very modest, are parked along every street in Saintes. The families meet up, make new friends, swap old stories and arrange marriages. Perhaps, because of its Mediterranean setting, or because of its truly international flavour, it seems even more colourful and exciting than most such festivals. For the gypsiologist, it is especially important as one of the few genuine gypsy meetings where there are no closed doors to the outsider. After the procession, watching gypsies dance round their fires, eating, talking and singing all together, is a stimulating experience. Not all Camarguais like the gypsy visitors. There is a lot of the usual talk about their thieving and breaking into cars, but overall the two spirits seem to be mutually compatible, for the gypsies keep on coming and the Camarguais keep on letting them. The biggest worry now is the fear that the number of visitors might be getting out of hand.

*Chapter 8*

# COWBOYS OF FRANCE AND THE SONS OF
# THE MISTRAL

---

"IN THE SOUTH of France, there where the Rhône throws itself into the sea, is a country that is almost deserted, called the Camargue, where herds of wild bulls and horses still live." So runs the script of *Crin Blanc*, the famous film of the area; and the dominant image of the Camargue, for the majority of its admirers and visitors, is not of bird-life or of farmers or of Provençals of some ancient order, but quite simply of an exotic wild country similar to that of America's West. It is seen as a romantic outpost, with white horses stampeding across the plains, their manes strung out in the wind, and fearsome black bulls weathering the cold winter in their stride. In some ways this picture is true. The bulls and the horses are there. They may be depleted in numbers, altered through crossing with other strains—though not yet too drastically—and exploited for their owners' livelihood, but they still manage to keep the dignity of centuries past and can enthrall the most hardened of cynical hearts when glimpsed knee-high in the marshes casting a disdainful eye at interloper man.

The Camargue is also well known as a land of cowboys, but it is difficult to find out just what this way of life actually involves. Camarguais are jealous of their traditions and secretive of their customs, but if you are a friend they may introduce you to a style of life that has not changed for the last couple of centuries, at least.

The number of bulls in the delta has varied considerably through the years. In the sixteenth century, Quiqueran de

Beaujeu estimated that there were some sixteen thousand bulls; during the Second World War the stock was almost eliminated and in 1961 the figure was six thousand. The German occupation was one of the hardest blows for the Camarguais who had to watch hundreds of bulls being slain for food or pleasure. Ironically, Goering was so fascinated by them that he took fifty back with him to try to breed wild bulls in Germany. No one knows what happened to them—unless they are still wandering the marshes and forests there. By 1944, there were one hundred and seventy-eight bulls and in 1945 only thirty-seven adults. After the War, the Camarguais began the slow and painful process of rebuilding the stock without weakening the strain. In the Petite Camargue, the Crau and the Greater Camargue today, there are fifty-five *manades* and, it is estimated, twelve thousand bulls.

The horses, too, are left in their wild state, though they are ridden by the *gardians* for work among the bulls. Today, there are probably no more than one thousand horses in the Isle of the Camargue, and up to three thousand in the total area; though Quiqueran de Beaujeu's sixteenth-century head count came up with a total figure of more than four thousand horses and mares. Any one *manadier*, today, keeps around twenty or twenty-five of the best horses for working purposes. These are the *manadiers* like Hubert Yonnet, of the Mas la Bélugue, who keeps Spanish and Portuguese strain bulls; Henri Laurent, of the Mas les Marquises, whose Camargue bulls are at present said to be the best; Marcel Mailhan, who is part-owner of four *manades*, and the well-known *manadière* Fanfonne Guillerme. Let us look more closely now at the animals they keep.

Where do the Camargue bull and horse come from? Are they really native of the area? Did they rise up out of the marshes along with primitive man and stay there over the centuries? Or did some ingenious person introduce them with an uncanny eye for what would appeal to twentieth-century man? Unfortunately these are not easy questions to answer, though many have tried.

The Camargue bull is a breed apart. It is small and lively,

long rather than tall, has a small head with pointed muzzle, lyre-shaped horns that point upwards rather than outwards, has a thick brown coat, runs lightly and fast and is altogether different from its Spanish or Portuguese brother. It lives in a herd, usually all male, for the females bring up their young in a separate group. It allows humans to approach to within about forty yards and a human on horseback can come within five to ten yards. Very rarely would a Camargue bull attack a horse. They don't like humans, understandably, but unlike the Spanish and Portuguese strain, their instinct is not to charge but rather to scamper away. The whole tradition of the Provençal bull games is dictated by the character of the animal.

How the bull came to be in the Camargue is another question. It is claimed to be direct descendant from prehistoric bull, *aurochs*, the species which finally became extinct in Europe in the seventeenth century after the last one had been killed in Lithuania in 1627. *Aurochs*, in turn, was descended from *bos primigenius*, a creature from the quaternary period. But does that mean that this primitive species survived in the Camargue because it was the last outpost of civilisation in Europe? or that it was imported from Asia Minor, one of the grand Asiatic race of wild bulls who roamed the plains? or that it was introduced by the Greeks? Opinions differ, though le Marquis de Baroncelli-Javon, mentor of the Camargue in the early part of this century, who took it upon himself to build up the stock of pure Camargue bulls, firmly believed that they were part of the Asiatic race that came to the Camargue after the Ice Age, when the warmer climate and encroaching hostility of man made their lives unstable. He believed that *aurochs* took refuge in the impenetrable marshes and forests of the Rhône delta, "fleeing before the hostility", it came to "a fantastic country where the silence of other eras reigned in the basin of marshes, the thick cover of reeds and depths of the forests. It still seems prehistoric and the destiny of these bulls never ceased to be of a noble race."*

* Marquis Folco de Baroncelli-Javon; *L'Élevage en Camargue de Taureaux*.

D

His fellow poet and comrade, Joseph D'Arbaud, continued to strengthen this notion about the bulls, in his story *La Bête du Vaccarès*. He put these words into the mouth of the half-human beast:

> Why do you pursue me, why have you set up this hunt, on horseback, and armed with your *trident*? This region is the last where I have been able to find a little peace and that sacred solitude which used to reign when I was master of the silence and of time, and master of the eternal song. Here, crossing the salty wastes, cut up by lagoons and sandy strips, listening to the bellow of bulls and the cry of wild stallions . . . I have known a time which for me almost resembles happiness. Yes, happiness . . . I have been happy, broken up as I was, crippled and defeated, in this desolate region which provided me at least with the means of protecting my aging body, but which also lent me the breath of the wild without which I could not live and for which I have fled gentler prairies, orchards in flower, and warm beaches . . . poor man. Yet look how you have impatiently followed me, for days on end, over this ground, how you are armed to trap and hunt me cruelly as if I were a ferocious beast to be conquered for your own miserable rewards. My peace and my sad happiness, are they finished now because, this evening, a man regards me face to face? Well, answer me. What do you want of me?

It's a symbolic tale of the pressures on the primitive world. But then, Baroncelli-Javon himself immortalised the mystery of the bull in one of his poems. ("I am the bull who from Asia to the Ligurian forests has reigned with joy through Art and through Blood over the Mediterranean peoples.")

> Je suis le taureau qui, depuis l'Asie
> Jusqu'aux forêts de Ligurie,
> A régné la joie, par l'Art et par le Sang
> Sur les peuples meditérranéens.*

\* Marquis Folco de Baroncelli-Javon: *Blad de Luno*.

The horses of the Camargue, it is as strongly believed, were also in the delta long before man. And they certainly look more like a prehistoric horse than any other you see roaming the fields or bridle paths of Europe. They have a mysterious expression, have stumpier legs and wide, low-slung bellies. They are small and solidly built, seldom above thirteen-and-a-half hands. They have strong, muscular necks and legs, hard hooves that do not need shoes, a long mane and tail, a wide flat brow, deep-set eyes and wide nostrils. The foals are born with a black or dark brown woolly coat, which gradually turns an iron grey and then fades until it becomes the adult pale grey or white. The horses look noble and proud and have a very pronounced streak of independence.

The southern area of France is dotted with caves containing paintings of horses, and the Camargue variety does seem to correspond to *Equus caballus robustus*. They could have come from the Central Asian steppes with the earliest human migrations, or might have been introduced relatively late by the Saracens. It is generally felt, however, that there were horses in the delta at the time of the Romans—though the horse games of Provence most resemble those of the Moroccan tribes of Tuaregs, which would have been a later influence. Of course, many of the so-called Camargue horses of today are a mixture of breeds, but interestingly enough, not the ones used by the ranchers for long and arduous work among the bulls. Cross-breeding was introduced to extend and perhaps improve the stock. But only the genuine Camargue strain could withstand the wild, the semi-aquatic life, the shortage of nourishing food, the work among the bulls and the long, tiring rides expected of them.

But bull and horse roamed free for several centuries before man realised their potential. The Ligurian tribes merely feared and kept their distance from the bulls. It would have been the Greek settlers who first taught the native tribes that the horses could be used to go among the bulls. The Romans were presumably the first to introduce the horse games into the arena, and the rise of the *course libre*, as I have shown in Chapter 2, is a practice that grew steadily from at least the Dark Ages. The *manadiers* who began to settle in the *sansouire* region of the Camargue in the late eighteenth and early nineteenth centuries, developed styles and traditions that are still adhered to today. We will start again with the bull, as he forms the focus of the Provençal passions which have led to the Provençal saying *la fé di biou*—one of the strongest motivating forces of this unique area.

When the Camargue bull enters the arena, he is virtually ignorant of human existence, though he has had one traumatic experience at man's hand (the *ferrade*) which he would not have forgotten. Basically, though, the bulls live wild in the *sansouire*. They feed off the salty *salicornia*, in the uncomfortable scrub lands where there is no shelter from sun or frost and are exposed to ice and storms capable of wiping out whole herds in a single night. They live in herds; in fact if a bull gets split off from the herd in a storm, he is very likely to die in a frantic struggle to relocate the rest. The bulls were once very vulnerable to the innumerable *roubines* and holes that opened up beneath their feet, and a large part of the *gardian*'s job was just riding around the land every day checking that the bulls had not fallen into trouble. Now, though, fencing and more careful guarding means that although they are still left to wander at will, the danger of *roubines* is largely avoided.

In spring the cows separate from the herd and produce, and then rear, their young. Even the *gardians* often have no idea when a cow has given birth until the day a tiny figure emerges from behind a clump of tamarisk. The *gardians* keep a rough idea of how many calves are born each year and the young are watched till they are a year old. Then, as *anoubles*, they are rounded up and branded. At the *ferrade* (branding), the *manadier* notes the young bull's character and potential based on how he conducted himself in the ring. He has to guess how the bull will bear up as a sporting beast for the *course*. The *manadier* will be looking not only for the most nimble, but for the pluckiest and most showmanlike of his bunch. Not much sentimentality is lost on the way. If the beast looks like being a dud by the time it is a two-year-old (a *doublen*), then it goes to the slaughter house.

For those *manadiers* who raise Portuguese, or cross-bred Portuguese and Camargue bulls, the required type is different. This strain of bull is more solid and aggressive and they end up in the *corrida* either dead or victorious. They are reared in the same way: wild in the *sansouire*. Again the *gardian* can approach on horseback and, if he wishes, by car (for the bulls are frightened of automobiles), though cars are hardly practical in the *sansouire* for the water appears in the most unexpected places and the spiky *salicornia* is no friend to a shiny patina or shaky exhaust pipe. The Spanish bull is left alone until it is two or three years old and then it is tested out at a 'secret' meeting called a *tienta*, which the *manadier* holds in his own private arena in the late spring.

These bulls have only one chance in the arena; they do not come back for more next year as the Camargue bulls do: by late autumn, after the *corridas*, there are no more three-year-olds to be seen in the fields; they have all gone, in one fashion or another, to the abattoir (for that is where the bull ends up after the *corrida* as well). At a *tienta* the bulls take a simulated run round the arena, as one *tentador* picks the bulls, and another holds the cape. A stockbreeder may run through thirty bulls in any one year. It is an expensive occupation, yet they say they cannot breed enough to meet the demand of the *corridas*.

But to return to the Camargue bull, as we left him, a shivering, frightened *anouble* running back to the safety of the herd and the wide plains. Once the *ferrade* is over, he leaves the care of the cows and joins the males in the main herd, where he lives for the next two years untouched by human interference except occasional moving to find better pasture. His next big adventure could be in summer, when the *sansouire* has dried up and the supply of *salicornia* with it, for the *manadier* may decide to move his bulls from the delta. This is the occasion for another Wild West scene, as men, horses and bulls move slowly westwards from the Camargue and northwards towards the pasture of Le Cailar in the Petite Camargue. The trek takes four or five days and is much loved by *gardians* and *cavaliers* (amateur *gardians*) alike and was once, at least, the warm-up to a summer of mad days and crazy nights when young and unattached cowboys lived it up in frontier fashion.

With the winter comes the long trek back and the bulls' battle against the elements begins again. One *manadier*, Henri Aubanel, described how, in the winter of 1941, a storm killed fifty-two bulls in one night. The next day they found corpses up to twenty kilometres away where the bulls had run to find cover. One corpse was found under a metre of snow and a cow was frozen to death standing up. When a bull dies, the rest of the herd join in an eerie bellowing, called *ramadam*, telling bulls all over of the sad fate. The *gardians* usually burn the corpse as the smell of blood and death frightens the herd.

Before the *ternen* (the three-year-old) reaches the *course*, he has to suffer one further indignity: castration. A non-castrated male is usually a failure in the ring: surprising, perhaps, for an animal so representative of a Latin *machismo*-dominated culture. The operation is called *le bistournage* and takes place in the autumn. The bull does his best to fight it and has to be tied up. Quite often the *gardians* provide a stuffed sack for the bull to charge immediately after the operation. Only one male is kept for breeding.

Once he has entered the ring, however, the bull is on his way to becoming a folk hero. The development of the *course libre* into the popular show it is today seems to have been sparked off by the partnership of a spectacular bull, *Le Sanglier*, and Rey, a popular *razeteur*. It was Rey who first introduced the uniform of the long white trousers and white shirts. *Le Sanglier* appeared on sixty memorable occasions between 1919 and 1930. Prizes on his *cocardes* were worth up to three hundred pounds—astronomical for those days—and up to a hundred pounds was given to anyone who could touch his forehead. Such adulation has never quite been seen since, though other bulls such as *Lou Vovo* and *Le Clairon* have also become household names. *Le Sanglier* died of old age in 1933 and his tomb is a favourite haunt of pilgrims.

Now that the *course libre* and the *ferrade* are well established there is little danger of the Camargue bull being cross-bred out of existence. That was a danger, though, once, and the stock bred in the Camargue is still protected by a group of *manadiers* known as the Association of Rearers of Bulls of the Camargue Race. Now, of course, the *manadiers* can choose which type of bull they wish to breed. Good stud bulls are shared around—"good" meaning not so much for the tenderness of the steak but for the agility with which they can leap a wooden barrier. The association has twenty-seven *manadiers* and some six thousand bulls under its auspices.

Let us now turn to the horses, for they inspire no less love and devotion. They are sometimes to be seen being rounded up by the sea, but these are usually the horses kept for rides and not the ones used by the *manadiers*. More often, they are found grazing among the marshy reeds by an *étang*, galloping in some stampede as hundreds decide that they must follow their leader round the edge of the lagoon or, more calmly, waiting in a corral for the next tourist ride. Tourism and commercialism have spoiled the horses in some ways, but one thing is sure: very few of the genuine, pure-bred Camargue horses will ever lose their dignity on tourist rides. These horses are rare, valuable and are jealously guarded by the *manadiers* for their own use, for the Camargue horse is a fine work horse.

The concern for preserving horses is as strong as it is for the bull, and there is a thriving Association of the Race of Camargue Horses. They hold an annual meeting where stallions are shown with as much pride and dignity as any British racehorse owner might take—even though the Camargue horses can scarcely bring in the same financial returns.

Though they are hardly likely to be left to starve, the horses of the Camargue do live wild. The infertile marshes are their feeding grounds and they are well adapted to the water, to the icy winters and the mosquito-infested summers. Occasionally they are stabled and fed by the *gardians* if the natural food supply is short, or if they are in need of special care only possible under cover. Unfortunately, the horses are very greedy animals, and

quite easily corrupted. A bag of grain will soon persuade a wild
horse to eat out of your hand, and the horses that are ridden
regularly certainly put away more sacks of grain than is good
for them. They tend to get fat bellies anyway, as the sparse
fodder of the Camargue is short on protein. But their instincts
are very sure and they are blessed with an infallible sense of
direction. On returning from a ride with the *gardians*, some
kilometres away from the herd and before the human eye can
distinguish them, the horse will suddenly snuffle, twitch his ears
and let out a loud whinny, recognising his return to his fellows.

When it comes to taming and training the horses, the
Camargue is very different from the American West. There is
no story of rodeos and bucking broncos here. The training of
the horse is very much a part of the whole ethic, based on love
for the animal and letting the human take second place. During
the breeding season, the horses are usually found in groups of up
to twenty mares to one stallion. Only the males are used as
work horses as the mares are in foal for eleven months of the
year. At a year old, the foals are branded, sometimes along with
the *anoubles* at a *ferrade*—though branding foals is a much more
delicate operation for they have long, spindly legs and a nervous
disposition and careless handling could result in a broken leg.
Sometimes, they use a lasso on the foals now, though that was
only introduced from America by Buffalo Bill when he brought
the Wild West Show to the Camargue.

The foal is lassoed, pulled to a standstill and a rope is tied
round its front and back legs. Then several *gardians* pull its legs
from underneath it, and the animal falls on its side. The foal is
very frightened. Its head has to be held down, its tail is pulled
between its back legs, and it is thus completely immobilised.
The *manadier* puts his mark on the foal; there is no need for a
number as he knows his horses by name. The tough little
animals then go back into the wild until they meet up again
with man. And they remember that first experience, no less than
do the bulls.

The attitude towards training the horse is one of patience
and tolerance, and loving care. Training begins when a horse

is four years old. The previous years' freedom should ensure the animal has strength and stamina. The *gardian* begins by just talking to the horse, and touching it gently, caressing it and generally getting it used to the idea of human presence. He'll move round the horse from left to right and then put it on a loose rope. Saddling is begun at this stage by using an old sack and then a light saddle, then a saddle and stirrups, and finally bags hung on the stirrups to simulate legs banging the horse's sides. All this takes several weeks.

The same *gardian* who has been working so patiently with the horse will mount him one day. If he's thrown off, he must get back on. Camargue horses do have a memory and, however bad the fall, they have to be remounted immediately. The cheekier horses may go into a spin, race off at a gallop or charge into the water—anything to rid himself of the encumbrance. There are some who are so fiery (and they are even more loved) that most people would avoid them; yet even they can prove faithful and obedient to one special rider. Once mounted, the *gardian* will then walk up and down, teaching the horse to obey the loose pull on the reins for left and right. The Camargue style is for long, loose riding, not strictly disciplined for either horse or rider. The horse's final classes are among the bulls—whom he already knows.

Once trained, the horse is kitted out in Camargue fashion. The saddle is the most notable of his effects. It is a working saddle made from carefully hand-tooled leather and will cost at least a hundred pounds. The style is taken from the old French saddle of the *gens d'armes* and has a high pommel in front, two pockets, and a raised cantle at the back. It holds the rider's legs away from the horse's body, making his knees stick out awkwardly. To the uninitiated this saddle can be very uncomfortable, but in ground that suddenly slips away into hollows, or is often knee-deep in water, it is a saddle of convenience. The stirrups are long and have covered feet; not easy to slip out of if a shrub or tree gets in the way, but, for legs sticking out so awkwardly, necessary. For the rest, the horse has a bridle and bit, long reins, a *caveçon*, a martingale which goes between

its front legs to the girth; and a crupper, attached to the back
of the saddle and looped under the horse's tail, to prevent the
saddle slipping forwards. Finally, there is the *seden*, a rope made
from the horse's own mane (or *crin*) and tail hair, which is
wound with a red cord and used, especially on an unsaddled
horse, for free riding, and at the *ferrades* for tying up the foal's
legs. The *seden* is as much a part of Camarguais tradition as is
the *trident*: the *gardian*'s final piece of decoration. A horse fully
kitted out can be carrying twenty kilos of weight, without his
rider, yet still can travel for days and kilometres on end. Even
so, only horses used for the tourists' rides are shod—and then
only the front two feet have shoes on. During the trek to take
the bulls to the pasture at Le Cailar, the horses manage two
hundred and fifty kilometres in five days. In 1905, the Marquis
de Baroncelli-Javon and a friend travelled by horse to Lyons,
covering three hundred and eleven kilometres in only forty-two
hours. And that was at walking pace, averaging seven kilometres
an hour. Stories about animals abound in the Camargue—
about their favourite horses—such as *Sultan*, the Marquis's
horse, who, on that journey to Lyons, was fourteen years old
and was carrying sixty-six kilos in weight. *Sultan* was the son of
an even more famous mare, *La Sultane*, who died at thirty-three
years old—and the year before her death she had travelled one
hundred kilometres in a day.

And so we come to the *gardians* or *cavaliers*, the cowboys or
horsemen. Firstly, they are not simple cowhands, nor do they
match the cinema's image of the cowboy; but are at once something more romantic and more peculiar to France. For some
they symbolise imagination and fantasy: a race of men apart.
They are more like the *vaquero* of Spain than the cowboys of
America who deal with more peaceful herds. The *gardians* have
certainly been in existence for centuries, being established in the
sight of the church and the law, with the founding of their
association, or fraternity, in 1512. Whatever state *gardianage*
fell into in the intervening years (and it did degenerate), the
spirit has always remained the same. All *gardians* are members
of the Antique Confrérie des Gardians de Taureaux et de

Chevaux de Camargue (or, in Provençal, Antico Counfrarié di Gardian de Saint-Jorge) and the archives in Arles show that this, one of the most ancient societies in France, was founded on 2nd January 1512, in the church of Saint George, their patron saint.

The aims of the fraternity were to provide mutual help in times of need and this is still really the case (though now it tends to be for a guard of honour at weddings and funerals). The *gardians* and their families have always been poor people, having opted for the simple country life, and enjoying freedom of spirit rather than concerning themselves with money and the glories of civilisation. These days it is considerably harder for *manadiers* to find reliable and good men who want to do the work, now that it is more difficult to live on love and the spirit alone. There is still very little money in being a *gardian* and although the image of them in their Provençal/Camargue costume, on saints' and festival days, is colourful and romantic, it is not the real picture. On a normal working day the *gardian* wears any old clothes; on a Sunday or feast day he wears his wedding suit as that was the last good suit he was able to buy.

Yet there are still hundreds of members of the Confrérie. *Gardianage*, as an activity, has lost none of its appeal and a lot of *cavaliers* who had decided that they really had to find more lucrative employment, are now *amateurs gardians*. They are the ones seen at festivals and hard at work at weekends and in the holidays helping to train the horses, brand the bulls or take the trek to Le Cailar in the summer. They are not looked down on because they can ride a horse, handle a *trident* and cope with the bulls as well as the next. The Confrérie has now introduced different categories of *gardian* to account for the change.

The *amateur gardian* might even have a *cabane* for weekend visits, for the reed huts still standing, once the traditional home of the lonely *gardian*, are not so popular for full-time use now. They are simple huts made from indigenous materials in an area where stone was only imported at great expense for the boss's *mas*. Most of the original *cabanes* have disappeared, and many were destroyed to make way for town or factory. Some newer ones have gone up as holiday homes, some are jealously guarded and preserved by artists or genuine *cavaliers*.

The *cabane* looks just like an upturned boat, with one rounded and one flat end. The rounded end always faces north-west, turning its shoulders on the cold *mistral*. The huts are small, being eight to twelve metres long and four or five metres wide. They are made up of two rooms: a living and kitchen area and a bedroom. The old *cabanes* would have been made of bundles of reeds overlapping each other, with a plaster strip on the top of the roof and a cross at the northern apex. Inside was a mud floor, and the barest of necessities; just the *gardian*'s equipment round the walls and a fire to sit and dream before. Like plains-people anywhere, they know solitude and respect privacy, but they also know how to enjoy themselves when together. They seem to reflect the way of life that dates back to the time of Louis XII, and certainly, there is a decided medieval ring in some of the festivals. Of course, the Camarguais, who are often born and bred in the saddle, are very good horsemen and women and show their paces on such occasions as the "day of the *gardians*", held near St George's day.

It is incredible to an outsider that, if the "day of the *gardians*" has to be called off because of the weather, it is so easily transferrable to another time and date. For it is quite a show. The *gardians*, in their smart costumes, ride from centres like Les-Saintes-Maries-de-la-Mer and they all converge on the arena in Arles. Thousands are there to watch the spectacle, for some very fine and exciting riding takes place—and some fun and games. The horse "games", as they are called, are action packed and full of history. In the arena of Arles, the best known are those like the "game of the ring and lances" in which the *cavaliers* have to loop a half-inch-wide ring with a lance, while travelling at full gallop. This game is mentioned in a manual of equitation dating from the seventeenth century. In the "game of the scarves", *cavaliers* in two teams are distinguished by wearing coloured scarves on their arms. The scarves are trophies that have to be taken by members of the other team with their *tridents*. It is not so much the speed that is important in this race,

A group of
Camargue horses

A Camargue bull alone in the salicornia on the Mas de Grand Romieu

A Spanish bull, also bred in the Camargue, on the Mas la Bélugue

as quick thinking. The game was reportedly played in the four-teenth century in front of Queen Jeanne at Avignon and, at Arles, before Benoit XIII on the marriage of Louis of Provence and Princess Yolande. The popes of Avignon, it seems, particularly enjoyed the Camargue horse games.

In the "game of the oranges", six young Arlesiennes stand in twos, one holding a tray and one a bag of oranges. This is where the fun begins. The *cavaliers* ride past the girls and with one hand try to take an orange and put it on the tray. What they miss goes to the crowd. The most exciting, though, is the "game of bouquets". It is similar to the one with the scarves, but more violent. A group of girls stand holding bouquets of flowers; one *cavalier* approaches, salutes and is given flowers while two or three others, called *les éperviers*, try to snatch it off him. If they succeed, they get a kiss. Medieval Provence *must* have been full of romance. Finally, there is "musical chairs", when *cavaliers* jump from horse to chair, racing against each other, as there is always one chair short. In the good old days, there used to be a horse race round the town, starting and finishing in the grand Boulevard des Lices; that kind of unwarranted licence doesn't fit in the Arles of today though.

And how the *cavaliers* love their horses. Each one remembers every horse he has ever ridden; and all know the names of Baroncelli-Javon's famous steeds: like *Sultan*, *Le Pape*, and *Rouge-de-Virgile*. Once an application was made to Paris for the Legion of Honour to be awarded to a horse, *Le Fouquet*, who had saved seven men from the sea. But Parisians have no under-standing of the Provençal mind and the award went not to *Le Fouquet* or to his *gardian*, but to the coastguard who had helped in the rescue—and who hadn't even got his feet wet. This is just one of the Camargue's little tales. "We love our horses," says a typical *amateur gardian* unashamedly, "and cry for them when they die."

Yet, would any of these traditions have continued to exist without the intervention of the poet and mythologiser who cemented the history firmly as part of a national identity? The

Camargue, in a way, was invented (or re-invented) for the Camarguais by its poets, like Baroncelli-Javon, following in the path of the great Provençal poet Frédéric Mistral. It was Baroncelli-Javon who gave Camarguais their mirror and they woke up to an awareness of their own glory. Camarguais could be playing a charade, a fancy dress game of their past life; they could just be dreamers, the Confrérie de Songeurs, as some call it; or they could be genuine visionaries with imagination enough to hold on to their past. Who can tell at this stage? Their own awareness was only heightened in the last part of the nineteenth century and early half of the twentieth, at the time of the great romantic revival; the Provençal renaissance would not have bloomed without Frédéric Mistral. His story must come first. The Camargue of today owes a lot to his creative imagination.

## Chapter 9

## POETS AND PEASANTS

THE NAME MISTRAL is better known to northern Europeans as the violent and tiring wind that comes to spoil a Mediterranean summer holiday; to very few northerners is the name associated with poetry. Yet Frédéric Mistral received a Nobel prize for his patriotic poetry at the age of seventy-four, and by the time he died ten years later was venerated not only throughout Provence but by some of the literary élite in Paris as well. His poetry brought life to a dying feeling of separatism, resuscitated the history of a people, and the language of one of the earliest civilisations in western Europe. It celebrated a past way of life and, while not exactly trying to stop the clock, it made a bid for continued separatism from the "machine worshippers" of Paris. If Mistral were not so unremittingly romantic he might even find a revival today, as his ideas fit so well the rural-revivalism found particularly in our industrialised societies. All today's talk of self-sufficiency, of living without the trappings of urban life, were hinted at by Mistral and actually practised by one of his most faithful disciples, le Marquis de Baroncelli-Javon, who took Mistral's credo to the Camargue. In the history of Provence, the Camargue always takes a special place.

Frédéric Mistral felt he had unusual and auspicious beginnings since he was born of a marriage between a patriarchal father and a very young girl. There was something meaningful about the meeting of this elderly man and the sixth daughter of a local mayor whom he first saw gathering wheat. Frédéric's father was thirty-five when he married young Delaïde, and their

first child was Frédéric, born on 8th September 1830 and
nearly called Nostradamus after the notable ancient who had
reputedly lived in their village of Maillane. Frédéric was the
light of his mother's eyes, and she in turn became the light in
his. He wrote about his parents, later in his life, in his autobiographical sketches, *Mes Origines.*

My parents were yeomen, and belonged to those families
who live on their own land and work it from one generation
to another. The yeomen of the country of Arles form a class
apart, a sort of peasant aristocracy, which, like every other,
has its pride of caste. . . .

We worked the land with four yoke of oxen, and kept a
head-carter, several ploughmen, a shepherd, a dairy woman
whom we called "aunt", besides hired men and women
engaged by the month according to the work of the season,
whether for the silk-worms, the hay, the weeding, the harvest
and vintage, the season of growing, or that of olive gathering.

How joyous it was, this atmosphere of rustic life. Each
season in turn brought its round of labour. Ploughing, sowing,
shearing, reaping, the silk-worms, the harvest, the threshing,
the vintage and the olive gathering, unrolled before my eyes
the majestic acts of the agricultural life, always a stern hard
life, yet always one of calm and freedom.

In Mistral's celebration of the rustic life lay the roots of the
renaissance. He mythologised the life of the French peasant in a
way no other French writer had done before him (French
literature seems to be predominantly that of the aristocracy
and courtly life). But his influence went deeper than that.
Maillane is a typical Provençal village to the north of Arles; it
is still a sleepy, backwater French village, housing a little
museum in the old Mistral family house. There, young Frédéric
learned to tell nursery stories and tales picked up around the
house in his native Provençal language. Langued'oc, the
ancient language of the area known as Provence and Languedoc,
was given that name by the Roman settlers. It is regarded by

outsiders as a *patois* because each village has a different dialect; but it is the old language of the area, which sounds like Spanish and looks like a mixture of Latin, Greek, Celtic, and some North African language. It did not die out as the native language of the area until long after Provence joined France in the fifteenth century, and French was only declared the official language in Avignon in the mid-sixteenth century. Langued'oc was, until then, the language of both pope and peasant. It was the history of the language that began to inspire the young Mistral as he journeyed through school and university in Avignon and hopefully dabbled in the art of poetry. While a student he met Joseph Roumanille, a teacher and the peasant son of a gardener, who was already writing poetry in Provençal and encouraging other poets to do so too. "Up to that time," writes Mistral, "I had only read a few stray scraps in Provençal, and it had always aggravated me to find that our language . . . was used only in derision."

Roumanille had read the poetry of the *troubadours*, the poets of medieval Provence, who had travelled and sung their rhymes to the people. It was this spirit that encouraged him. He was struck by the effect of the language when written in that old style. There was already the beginnings of a renaissance movement in Marseilles, and Roumanille had his first verses published in a new Provençal journal called *Boui-Abaisso* (1841–6). All the Provençal literary magazines deliberately underplayed their importance by choosing commonplace names: the *bouillabaisse* is a Provençal fish-soup. Later, in 1855, Roumanille set up his own printing press and published the Journal *Armana Prouvençau*, which became immensely popular. Alphonse Daudet, author of *Letters from my Windmill*, described how his family was "exiled" in Lyons: "We used to go and wait for the 'Armana' when it came in, as men in the colonies look out for the mail boat from France."

Roumanille, Mistral and then a third friend, Anselme Mathieu, were the three men who, when Mistral was only twenty-two years old, founded the Midi's answer to Paris's *Académie*, in the *Félibrige*, an association of Provençal poets. The

*Félibrige* still exists and card-carrying members continue to subscribe to the ideal of perpetuating the culture of Provence, of keeping the language and customs alive. Why the association was called the *Félibrige* is something of a mystery, except that the title came from Mistral's reading of the story of the young Christ's meeting with the seven doctors of law, *les sept félibres de la loi.* Mistral claimed it had no particular meaning, but the symbolism of seven (Mistral has seven letters, there were seven poets, and there is a vague association with the seven sorrows of Our Lady) has been noted by critics. But they all liked the name and pursued it further by inventing a new language from it: *félibre* was to be a brotherhood of poets, *félibrige* the work of the association, and they all took nicknames, *le félibre de . . .* something or other.

Mistral, by this time, had taken his degree at Avignon and had decided to return home to the lowly *mas* to help his mother on the land, as his father was now nearly eighty and blind. Of course, Mistral was also to find inspiration from the land. He wrote, "We no longer think of Paris, in this time of innocence, while at Arles I have on my horizon, as Virgil recognised with Mantone, poetry in my surroundings—my far off ambition." He had no lowly vision of himself, though, and saw his rôle as the Homer of Provence. And his inspiration came. It was while he was watching the labourers working and singing that the first words of *Mireille* came to him. *Mireille* eventually became a twelve-canto poem, written of course in Provençal, telling the story of a young peasant girl in love with Vincens; she is being courted by three other young men, all of whom are encouraged by her father while Vincens is definitely not. She rejects all suitors and weeps for Vincens. Lovesick and forlorn, she rushes off to the Camargue to seek help from the Holy Marys; but she suffers under the pitiless sun in the delta, and dies tragically as the Marys appeared before her eyes. It is a poem that sings with high romance, contains some beautiful lines and is certainly the best evocation of Provençal life, and of the Camargue in its austerity and beauty.

Mistral's own relationship with the Camargue is interesting,

as some people say he had never visited the area before writing
*Mireille*. It must have been a voyage of discovery and revelation for him, for no one else had ever read so much into the
desolate wastes. In his autobiography, though, he describes
how he and Mathieu joined the pilgrimage to Les-Saintes in
1855, leaving Beaucaire with a party of fellow travellers in a
horse-drawn wagon. On this trip, he met a young girl, who
was nursing a broken heart which, according to her mother,
was driving the girl insane. Mistral relates how a storm blew up
over the Camargue and flooded the road, and how he had to
lift her through the mud—an act of mercy which he enjoyed
considerably. Critics have claimed that this was the moment
when his inspiration came symbolising Provence in the image
of Mireille, to whom Mistral had literally given new life.
(Unfortunately the same critics do not discuss the significance
of the young girl's death.) It is from this poem, though, that we
can understand how readily the appeal of the Camargue could
spread; how stimulating it proved to be. Mistral himself wrote,
"What impresses me most is the harmonious grandeur of the
vast sweep of land and sea, arched over by the limitless dome
of sky, which, more perfectly than anywhere else, appears to
embrace the entire terrestrial horizon." And the lines in the
poem have that same sweep and majestic vision. I must quote
some. I have chosen the section on the horses kept by Mireille's
first suitor, Veran, who came, suitably enough, from Le Sambuc,
one of the tiny one-horse towns in the Camargue:

> A hundred steeds,
> With manes like billows of the sea,
> Long wavy thick and innocent of shears.
> And when they start impetuous
> On their headlong courses
> Their dishevelled manes fly up
> And like the scarfs of white-robed fairies wave.
>
> Oh! shame upon the human race!
> Camarguan steeds have never

To the cruel spur,
No more than to the hand that flatters them,
Been known to be submissive. . . .
And to their native Vaccarès returned
To breathe their salt-sea-air again, and roam
In freedom after ten years' slavery!

For those white horses' element's the sea!
Foam-coloured they are still!
They doubtless from the car
Of Neptune broke away!
For when the sea is heard to moan and seen to scowl,
When ships their cables part,
The stallions of Camargue rejoicing neigh,

And smack like whipcord
Their long-hanging tails,
Or paw the ground
As though they felt
The pricking trident of the angry god,
Who stirs the tempest into deluge
And the sea's depths to their very bottom.

Or there is the section on the *ferrades*:

. . . had sent into the wild
A hundred of their ablest horsemen
Roused in their salt-wilderness,
Pursued and harassed by the trident

Of the impetuous brander
At full gallop, bulls and heifers
Like a gust of wind came headlong
Rushing, crashing salicorne and centaury
And mustered at the branding booth,
Where crowds had met,
Three hundred strong.

Branding at a *ferrade*

The *triage* at a *ferrade*. *Gardians* driving bulls into the *bouvau* for branding

It's both strongly narrative and lyrical, and despite what it obviously loses in translation, and the same goes for its translation into French from the original Provençal, of course, you can see how seriously he took his rôle as the Homer of Provence.

*Mireille* had taken Mistral seven years to complete, and when published by his friend Roumanille in 1859, on his own presses, Mistral sent it to the famous Lamartine in Paris and won instant fame and credibility for these "rustic" verses. It was Lamartine who hailed him loudest and claimed that his poem was about Provence itself rather than simply a love story. Mistral was still only twenty-eight at the time and had already embarked on a much greater work was which aimed at restoring a sense of history and tradition among the Provençaux. The *Félibres*, despite Lamartine's support, were often mocked in Paris as a group of dreamers who took their wives on Sunday picnics when they spoke in *patois* and made speeches and poetry in Provençal. But, to Mistral, there was no pretension about his involvement. He was working on a great dictionary of the Provençal language, not only of the words but listing all the customs, habits, herbs, flowers, and costumes. *Le Trésor du Félibrige* is an epic work. It contains all the words of Langued'oc in seven different dialects, each one compared with the original Latin tongue, and translated into French, plus all the proverbs and idioms of the south. It was finally printed in 1874 on two thousand four hundred closely printed pages, after twelve years of work. But then Mistral had said, "Even if I have to give twenty years of my life to it, I will undertake to show that our speech is a language, not a dialect, and I will reconstruct the laws on which it was once formed."

Mistral survived the years and his great age added to his popularity; though it is hard to imagine these days the hysterical adulation that could surround a poet, drawing huge crowds into the arenas to hear him speak and read his poetry. As the voice of the people, a poet of ordinary folk, he held a position similar to that of a pop star or folk singer of today. He wrote many other poems, such as *Calandel* and *Le Poème du Rhône*, all written firstly in Provençal and only later translated into French.

The Revolution in Paris hardly affected the southerners except to increase the ardour of their nationalism and the appeal of arch-chauvinist Mistral. He was courted by other writers, even followed by one aristocratic Irishman, William Bonaparte Wyse, who visited him as a pilgrim, stayed and became fluent in Provençal. In 1904, Mistral received ten thousand francs as the Nobel prize for patriotic literature, for *Mireille*, and he used the money to set up a museum dedicated to the Provençal way of life. The Muséon Arlaten still stands in Arles as Mistral left it. It is popular but confusing to tourists as it is crammed with every possible Provençal gadget under one dark and gloomy roof.

Even in his seventies, there was no stopping the patriarchal figure. He started his own Provençal paper *L'Aïoli* (named after the Midi's garlic-flavoured mayonnaise), and took on his enthusiastic young disciple, Baroncelli-Javon, as assistant editor. Mistral's autobiographical sketches were published in 1904 and were greeted with garlands of praise, such as this adulation in *Semaine Littéraire de Genève*: "This exquisite, joyous, healthy, cheering book. This delightful picture of the Midi, with its honest country life, its ancient manners, preserved by a passionate attachment to the ancestral soil and example, calls forth laughter, smiles and tears. It is, perhaps, the most purely joyous, moving and charming, work that France has given us for a long time."

On 15th December 1904, Mistral received a letter from the American White House, signed by Theodore Roosevelt which said:

You are teaching the lesson that none need more to learn than we of the West, we of the eager, restless, wealth-seeking nations; the lesson that after a certain amount of material well-being has been reached, the things that really count in life are the things of the spirit. Factories and railways are good up to a certain point; but courage and endurance, love of wife and child, love of home and country, love of lover for his sweetheart, love of beauty in man's work and in nature, love and emulation of daring and lofty endeavour, the homely work virtues and the heroic virtues—these are better still, and if they are lacking, no piled-up riches, no roaring, clanging, industrialisation, no feverish and many-sided activity shall avail either the individual or the nation. I do not undervalue these things of a nation's body; I only desire that they shall not make us forget that beside the nation's body there is also the nation's soul.

Mistral makes nonsense of the common belief that a poet rarely receives honour in his own time and his own country. At the end of the last century (from 1873) when the French government persisted in keeping the arenas closed to both Provençal and Spanish bullfights, the people of Nîmes arranged a bullfight in defiance of the government. Mistral made his own personal decision to attend, thereby risking a fine, and as he entered, the crowd of twenty thousand stood and cheered and chanted his name. "In the south," he said to them, "the passion for bullfighting is more deeply rooted than in Spain itself." His death in 1914 was widely mourned, and his statue in Arles was miraculously saved by his faithful *Félibres* from destruction by the Germans.

Mistral lived all his life at Maillane in the *mas* of his parents and shunned sophisticated literary life. He maintained his links with Arles rather than with Avignon, even though he was very much sought after by Parisian and English intellectuals. Augustus John, who came to live in Martigues, then a small fishing village, once tried to obtain a sitting with the master, but was rather rudely turned away.

The second generation of *Félibres*, inspired by the ideas of Maillane, took Mistral's vision further into the country rather than away to the cities. When Folco de Baroncelli-Javon, for example, went to the Camargue, he actually renounced his worldly goods in true apostle style. Baroncelli-Javon thought that Mistral's ideas belonged with the rough, unsophisticated splendour of the peasant which he found in the Camargue rather than in the heady, sun-kissed slopes of Provence.

Baroncelli-Javon came from a family of Florentine aristocrats whose ancestry was long and uninterrupted but who, in
1840, had had to go and live in Provence. At the time, the
family were in the situation of decayed gentry; they had no
money and the mother had to make a living selling tapestries.
Folco was born in 1869, in the village of Bouillargues just outside
Avignon, where as a young boy he soon became familiar with
the horses of the area. He went to school in Nîmes, and stayed
just outside the town at a *mas* where, once summer had come, he
saw the *gardians* bringing the bulls and horses to the pastures of
Le Cailar. The excitement of that memory never left him.
Later, at school, he began to try to understand the southern
passion for bulls. He was already enthusiastic about the horses,
but the bulls were new to him. These passions of the Midi were
transformed into an obsession with Provençal poetry and, by
the time he had returned to Avignon, he was already fascinated
by the *Félibrige* and wanted to become one of them. Several
young poets and intellectuals had taken to meeting in the
Café de Paris, in Avignon. Alphonse Daudet came from Nîmes,
Charles Maurras from Martigues, Paul Arène from Sisteron,
and then there was the grand master Stephan Mallarmé.
Young Folco, then about twenty years old, was very much a
down-table poet, but with Joseph D'Arbaud and his friend
Marius André, he thrived on the inspiration of the older men.
When he and André wrote their first books (Folco's was a
story of a young girl called *Babali*), they symbolically threw a
copy into the Rhône, as the nourishing source of Provence.

It was on 6th January 1891 that Folco and Marius André
brought the first edition of *L'Aïoli* back from the presses.
Folco was already becoming something of a protégé of Mistral,
who made him assistant editor in charge of a secretary, the
choice of manuscripts, the page layouts and proofs. *L'Aïoli* came
out three times a month and Folco often went to Maillane,
where Mistral worked, to indulge in the long meal-time
discussions that took place there. Young Baroncelli-Javon was
already going to the Camargue every weekend to ride, when,
in 1890, at only twenty-one, he decided he had had enough of

the literary world of Avignon, the wealthy trappings and
potential glory of that life, and that he would cut his ties and go
and live in the Camargue.

He found that life there was still dictated by the poor earth,
that the *gardians* and fishermen expressed what they wanted to
say in their own peasant language without any educated
niceties, and that the whole way of life, centred round the bulls,
was the best way of supporting Mistralism. More than that,
Baroncelli-Javon could not help but notice that things were
changing. Every year more land was being reclaimed from the
northern part of the Camargue to plant cereals and vines, the
salt industry was growing and a new chemical factory had gone
up at Salin-de-Giraud. People even spoke of drying out
Vaccarès to make ultimate use of the land, which would have
meant the end of the wild bird life. Also, the thin and
scraggy bulls then reared in the Camargue were being crossed
with Spanish strain to obtain fatter animals for the butcher and
the pure Camarguais race of bull was dying out. So Baroncelli-
Javon took it upon himself to try to save these traditions.
He decided to live out his ideals rather than just build a reputation as a writer. When he told Mistral of his plan, the master
was not particularly encouraging, for he could not know how
far Baroncelli-Javon would identify himself with the Camargue:
"Je te confie la Camargue, Folco. Tu la connais mieux que
moi. Defends-là." ("I trust the Camargue to you, Folco. You
know it better than I. Defend it.") So, like an ancient *cavalier*,
Folco said goodbye to his friends and family, and all the
benefits of the big city, sold his worldly goods and took his horse
down towards Les-Saintes-Maries-de-la-Mer. He stayed there
for sixty years.

From the glamour of the *Félibrige* in Paris or Avignon,
Baroncelli-Javon was now to be seen in the Camargue, a small,
thin man, ill-fed, solitary and dressed in faded shirt and
moleskin trousers, with a red and white cord (the *seden*) round
his waist. On the walls of his *cabane* was written the motto of
the Crusaders: "God gives the earth to his faithful friends".
Baroncelli-Javon started life by renting the Mas de l'Amarée

near Les-Saintes, which included a *mas* building and a circle of *cabanes*. He started to build up a herd of pure Camargue bulls, for he was determined to breed back dignity into man and beast. And Baroncelli-Javon always set the shining example himself. With his move to the Camargue, he had left behind any vestiges of his aristocratic upbringing. He lived as a *gardian*, working all day, and many nights, taking no holidays or week-end visitors. He spent his days following the bulls, saving them from treacherous waterholes, and spotting the young as they were born. He was immediately respected and became known as *lou marques* (the Marquis), and not as *maître* as other bosses might have been. At nights, in the *mas*, a bare building with very little furniture and no ornaments other than the basic equipment used by a *gardian*, he would sit by candlelight writing up the record of his herd of two hundred bulls and fifty horses, like any good stockman. He would take his meals with the other *gardians*, and, in true Camargue fashion, they would eat without speaking a word. The *gardian* is used to the solitary, meditative way of life and is not given to chatter even over the meal table. Baroncelli-Javon had neither electricity nor water. Yet he managed to continue editing *L'Aïoli* from the Mas de l'Amarée, receiving word from the *Félibrige* by the train that then ran from Arles to Les-Saintes. He still wrote his own poems; maybe even more inspired by having realised his dream. And his first volume, *Blad de Luno* (*Blé de Lune*), is still the bible to some Camarguais, celebrating as it does the whole life of bull, horse and delta.

There were other poets around, from a similar background, who offered a little light relief and moral support: these men, such as Joseph D'Arbaud and Bernard de Montant-Mause together with Folco, would always lead any Provençal fête or special occasion, the *gardians* even, it is said, voluntarily doffing their hats. Part of the Provençal tradition, as President Theodore Roosevelt spelled out, was a firm Victorian belief in the family and the strength of loyal ties; and Baroncelli-Javon played his part here too. Mistral had re-inaugurated the *Festo Virginenço*, a Provençal custom, in Les-Saintes, and every year this extremely chauvinistic celebration of young maidens who had lived true to Provençal myth, custom and ideal, paraded in Arlesienne costume and received diplomas to endorse their virtue in spirit and deed. Baroncelli-Javon also started up a new association of *gardians*, to run conjointly with the ancient *Confrérie*, this one dedicated to upholding the dignity of Provençal dress and to the revival of the language. The *Nacioun Gardiano* was responsible for the full-dress turn-outs when a guard of honour of *gardians* was needed, and it was through them that the Provençal horse games were revived. If, sometimes, these fancy dress parades seemed like a charade, the Camarguais at the time did not let on. And Baroncelli-Javon went from strength to strength. Before his death, Mistral was able to revise his early thoughts and say, with tears in his eyes, "Folco, les ailes de ta foi planent sur les déserts salés plus hauts que celles de goëlands." ("Folco, the wings of your faith fly higher over the salt wastes than those of a gull.")

Baroncelli-Javon was an eccentric in a lovable amateur fashion; an interesting man about whom there is little known. The French novelist Henri de Montherlant made a reference to him in *The Matadors* (*Les Bestiaires*). Montherlant himself was entirely obsessed by *tauromachie* and was, some say, a relative of Baroncelli-Javon and this rather dry reference to the Marquis, which I shall have to quote as it is the only outside reference to Camargue affairs I have found, does add a wider perspective and gives one cynical view on this romantic revival.

The Marquis de X . . . belonged to an eminent Florentine family which had emigrated to Provence in the sixteenth century—one of them had a hand in the murder of Julien de Medici—and which kept a palace at Avignon dating from that time. At an age when others of his kind chase after heiresses or buy and sell car after car in pursuit of a mechanical ideal, the present Marquis had bought a small farm down in the Camargue and shut himself off from the world. Here he reared wild bulls for the local rings, treating it as his sacred duty to preserve the traditions and distinctive character of the people of the south of France.

This man who spent his days on horseback sharing the lives of his bulls and herdsmen was a poet—by his artistry one of the great poets of Provence, and by the life he led one of the great poets of France. . . . People of his own social status resented him because he did not blindly follow their own pattern of existence. It shocked them that he should make a living out of renting bulls—they would not have said a word against him had he gone from door to door selling life assurance . . . the Marquis tended to enjoy a smaller return than if he had stayed in town and bred pedigree pups from one of his own pet dogs, and he only just managed to make ends meet. Armed with a *trident* and clad in moleskin trousers, he was not even successful in becoming a notorious figure in Parisian eyes, since the literary set had long since taken up Provence in a big way and quite put him in the shade with their carefully shocking ties and dramatically wide-brimmed hats . . . they never spoke his name without prefacing it with the words "that fool . . ." just as they never mentioned Homer without calling him "old" Homer.

But according to still-living memories in the Camargue, he was a man who commanded not only respect but love. His sincerity was obvious and his ways were amusing. When he married, he surprised everyone by picking no "Mireille" or "Babali", but a sophisticated young lady from Paris whose parents arranged a honeymoon for the two of them in Nice, Monte Carlo, Capri and Sorrento. The train taking them away, however, stopped for two minutes at Arles station and Baroncelli-Javon said, "Shall we get down?" They did and his wife was taken back to his miserable *gardian's cabane*, where she bore him three daughters and presumably learned to adapt to the life. One daughter, Frédérique (known as Riquette), married Henri Aubanel, the son of a local family of *manadiers*, and, between them, they have taken over her father's work of keeping the traditions.

The story of his wedding is, perhaps, the least well known of Folco's eccentricities. More evident were his ideas and love for the gypsy nation that visited Les-Saintes every year. He became their honorary king, and fought on their behalf, and for other oppressed minority groups, from this strange vantage point. Just after the turn of the century his voice was heard in favour of the independence of the Boers in the war of the Transvaal; and he also denounced to European diplomats the systematic massacre of the Red Indians of the American West. Few of the eight hundred thousand there had been in 1800 survived and Baroncelli-Javon spoke for them in the name of all horsemen, who were to him "the first occupants of the soil". The Marquis expounded a theory that Indians and gypsies are of the same original nomadic race, as there are many similar words in their languages and they share religions based as the sun. He drew a picture showing them living together in the Bronze Age and claimed that a giant earthquake in the Atlantic Ocean created the geographical divide between them. According to him, their survivors on the oriental side of the Atlantic were the *fellahs* in Egypt, the gypsies from India and the Basques; and in the Americas themselves the Red Indians and the Incas. He published these ideas in a manifesto called *L'Âme Rouge*, which links them with the ancient cult of Mithraism, as a fire-god; and so with the Provençal cult of the bull.

Very few people took him seriously, though the actual work he did on behalf of the gypsies and Indians could not be doubted. He once rode all the way to Lyons on horseback to plead for the gypsies with a man intending to buy up an ancient mansion in which the gypsies had always met and were still using as a stopping place. The man refused and was warned about the gypsies' curse which would be put upon him. He was not to know that he would be killed by a car the next day. No one else bought the place, and the gypsies continued to use it.

But the strangest and most colourful incident, in Baroncelli-Javon's life, concerns the Red Indians. A member of the Confrérie de Gardians, in America, passed the Marquis's message of sympathy and understanding around and his words reached Buffalo Bill, later to become Colonel Cody, who arranged to visit Les-Saintes with his circus of Red Indians while on tour in Europe. The Indians were made very welcome by Baroncelli-Javon, they stayed with him at the *mas* and, as their stay coincided with the Les-Saintes festival (*Festo Virginenço* and horse games) that year, the Camargue had cowboys, *gardians*, and Indians in war dress competing in the equestrian acrobatics. The Indians set up their wigwams round the L'Amarée and the famous chiefs became close friends of the Marquis: Iron Tail; Chief Lone Bear, the war-god; Chief Red Cloud who was over a hundred years old; and the great Sioux, Chief Sitting Bull, who had fought at Little Big Horn and had scalped General Custer's army. When they left, the *mas* was decorated with tomahawks and feathered head-dresses and the Marquis received the honorary name of "Zind-Kala-Wasté", meaning faithful bird. In the museum to Baroncelli-Javon, a tiny tower-like building in the centre of Les-Saintes, some of those souvenirs and proud photographs of the chiefs are displayed, inscribed to the Marquis: "I give this photograph to my friend Zind-Kala-Wasté." In one photograph Baroncelli-Javon is dressed in full Indian costume.

But things cannot always continue at this idealistic level and as the years progressed, Baroncelli-Javon left his first rented home, the Mas de l'Amarée, and built himself a replica *mas*, which he called *Le Simbéu*, near to the sea, just one kilometre outside of Les-Saintes. The *mas* was named after the famous bull, *Le Simbéu*, but it literally means a "symbol", which, of course, the Marquis had always been for the Camargue. In 1940, the Germans occupied the Camargue and began to destroy some of the buildings by the sea for blockhouses, and Le Simbéu was one that went. Baroncelli-Javon was by now very old and he moved back to Avignon, depressed and sick. Just before he died he asked to ride back to Les-Saintes and with one of his former *gardians* he made the long ride there and back. The *gardian* was a man called André Dupuis, who had joined the Marquis as a sixteen-year-old and remembers him vividly. We shall come to more of his story later.

Baroncelli-Javon died in 1943, at the age of eighty-four.

His body was brought back to Arles from Avignon, by train, and then taken from Arles to Les-Saintes on the little Camargue train. There, at Les-Saintes, the funeral cortège was waiting and his casket was lifted on to the backs of twelve gypsies who made the long trek from Les-Saintes to the site of Le Simbéu where his tomb still stands; the crowd of gypsies and local inhabitants was surrounded by *gardians* and horsemen who loved him. To this day, the spirit of Baroncelli-Javon is celebrated in the spring, after the gypsy festival, with the "Jour Baroncellien" when a procession makes its way out to Simbéu.

Joseph D'Arbaud, author of *La Bête du Vaccarès* and contemporary of Baroncelli-Javon, had also given up the literary world of Aix and Avignon to retire to the Camargue. He, too, felt that the Camargue was the essential primitive land; that everything about it was Provençal in style and nature, but in an untouched state. Both D'Arbaud and Baroncelli-Javon had looked for something primitive that they could help preserve. The rigours of the Camargue nearly finished D'Arbaud though, for the dampness made him ill and eventually he had to leave for drier climes, though he did not die till 1950.

Like Baroncelli-Javon, whose poetry is widely respected for its command of the Provençal tongue, D'Arbaud was also a strong Mistralian who wrote in Provençal, though in his case some say the achievement was greater as he wrote in prose. Provençal is a language without many abstract words, which is why it adapts to the romantic song form used by the *troubadours*, yet D'Arbaud managed to relate stories, and there are several volumes of them, all immensely readable, rich in mystery and symbolism.

Joseph D'Arbaud was a second generation Mistralian, and his parents were a fairly literary and visionary couple. His mother was a *Félibre* who wrote poetry herself. She was the daughter of an erudite philologist who spoke Provençal. The family was noble and cultivated, yet spiritually still attached to earth, and Marie certainly saw in the *Félibrige* an escape from the modern world. Her son Joseph, after studying law at Aix, was also drawn back to the simple life on the delta. There, he was inspired by the silence and empty spaces, by Provençal love of mystery and the supernatural. He told his stories as if they were real legends, but all were the fantasies of his own mind. He lived the life of poverty, rode with the Marquis and was something of a recluse. Between them they produced a literature for the Camargue, which must be quite rare for an area so small.

They had a direct influence on younger men and women, but the Second World War which smashed up the *mas* Le Simbéu made a mockery of those simple ideas. How could a romantic revival exist in the post-war days? How could an association of men devoted to *not* progressing, calling each other nicknames and forever looking backwards, co-exist with the new baby, technology? It did not survive intact, and it was perhaps fortunate for the Marquis that he died of old age, rather than of disappointment. But, though the Camargue went on to be exploited for more agriculture and tourism, something of the old spirit remains. To see the effect that Baroncelli-Javon's way of life had on his contemporaries, is to understand something of that heritage that still burns in the Camargue.

# Chapter 10

## THEY RODE WITH THE MARQUIS

---

To help preserve the old way of life, René Baranger, a *gardian* who knew and worked with Baroncelli-Javon, wrote his own memoirs in a book called *Un An de Gardianage en Camargue*. Like so many *nouveaux gardians* of the time, Baranger was not of the area but was just passionate about horses and the life style. He had heard of Baroncelli-Javon and systematically sought him out, asking if there was a job going for him. René, then only fourteen, was obviously at an impressionable age, yet it is Baroncelli-Javon himself who writes with obvious emotion in the book's Preface (and by then he was in his seventies), "I would like to communicate to those who will read it, the shiver these recalled memories have caused in me and the deep joy with which I see the flame of Mithraism still burning so intensely on the altar". (Baroncelli-Javon was always a strong believer in the Mithraic cult.) All René knew was that at that time he wanted to live, "in the pure air of the plains, amid the wild bulls and one day to be capable of riding any of the horses".

He met the Marquis at the festival of Arles in 1926, and was grudgingly told to come back to the Mas de l'Amarée after the show, though Baroncelli-Javon recalls that he was not keen on having anyone so young riding with them. He was told to search out the *bayle-gardian* (chief *gardian*) and ask for work. So young René took the train from Arles to Les-Saintes. When he arrived, he could not find the *mas* and spent the night sleeping in a barn. Later, he walked up the *draille*, track, to the *mas* and was greeted by the Marquis' daughter, Riquette, wearing Arlesienne dress.

E

He was immediately sent out on horseback, bareback, to look for horses that had wandered down to the Rhône from the *segonal*, the uncultivated area between the river and the *sansouire* which acts as a natural dyke. René gradually became part of the Marquis' entourage; he describes the *ferrades*, and the journey to Le Cailar.

That long journey, taking five days or more, posed many problems. They moved hundreds of bulls and so needed plenty of *gardians*. When they crossed open spaces, things were all right, it was when they began to go through a tighter gap that the animals panicked. Leaving the Camargue, they crossed the ancient bridge at Sylvéréal, which was made up of boats. When they reached the meadows of Le Cailar, several *manades* met together to enjoy the summer months in the Languedoc with village *courses*, *abrivades* and horse games; wine, women and song. These were the real cowboys of France.

René Baranger only stayed a year, but he had had time to appreciate the life. He writes of the lonely evenings in the *mas*, when the Marquis would sometimes cook for them, and then quietly sit and keep up with his records; of winter evenings, when René would go down to the sea to watch "la mer dechainée" (the unbridled sea); and of sitting in the *cabane* in front of a tamarisk wood fire. Easing himself back into the atmosphere, he remembers an expedition organised by the Marquis to look for some lost animals. They all mounted their horses, with just a bedroll for comfort, and set off for who knows how many days. "J'eus un instant l'illusion d'assister au départ d'une de ces caravanes d'aventuriers qui, un demi siècle d'auparavant, s'engagaient courageusement dans les déserts inconnues de l'ouest Américain," he wrote. ("I had for an instant the illusion that I was taking part as one of those great bands of adventurers who struggled bravely with the unknown deserts of America's West, half a century ago.")

But there are other people still in the Camargue, living in some other manner now, who rode with Baroncelli-Javon and who regard the experience as one of the most important in their lives. André Dupuis is one such, who, as a professional, may be found showing parties of influential visitors or schoolchildren round the central pumping station of the big drainage scheme, known as the Bas-Rhône-Languedoc. As a young *gardian*, it was he who rode with Baroncelli-Javon from Avignon to Les-Saintes, in the year before the Marquis' death to look at Le Simbéu again. He joined Baroncelli-Javon as a *gardian* when he was only sixteen. After the war, he continued for another three years before giving in to the need to earn a better living. A self-confessed romantic, Dupuis really warms to his subject when asked about the Marquis.

He did not grow up in the Camargue. His parents were from Provence but were living on the Swiss border. As a young boy, André would come to the Camargue for his holidays and he grew to love the delta. His parents had both been *Félibres*, and André still carries his membership card proudly with him. Now a city person, he cherishes his simple childhood, in an area that had no roads, no cars and very few people. "I'm an incurable romantic though. I don't know if we should really dwell on all that any more," he says, "it's pages from a history book and perhaps we should be looking for tomorrow. I hardly ever go to Les-Saintes any more because it's so different now. Yet, I have my memories. I wouldn't wish to impose them, or that way of life, on anyone else though."

Dupuis is a handsome, youthful man, sitting in his office in Nîmes thirteen floors up in the only skyscraper in the area, giving him a commanding view of the Camargue. His paradoxical situation is that he is working for a company that has revolutionised the standards of living of the people to the west of the Camargue, by introducing successful drainage. That in itself was a feat of miraculous proportions, and, Dupuis hopes, one that means the area is changing for the best with the minimum of commercial exploitation. The drainage scheme will not reach the Camargue proper, as the situation there is so different. To the west of the Camargue, though, in the Petite Camargue and Languedoc areas, there were miles of swamps, marshes, and sandy soil with no water for growing crops. It was impossible to build towns or villages as there was no drinking water; yet, ironically, the area was bordered by hills with natural streams carrying water by the gallon right past their very noses. A drainage scheme was finally devised by Philippe Lamour, a lawyer and journalist, who came from Paris to live in Nîmes after the war. He was a natural inventor and was working on a way to bring irrigation to the area when he found the papers of one Aristide Dumont, a local engineer whose plans had been begun in the last century, but let slide through lack of support.

Lamour received state aid with little difficulty, but initially met with local opposition. Farmers did not like the idea of having to put up money for this scheme. By the time it was working, however, they all rushed to join in. The company of Bas-Rhône-Languedoc, set up in 1955, is now a vast concern which advises on an international level (Kruschev insisted on visiting it on his tour in 1960). On a local level it has taken over the responsibility for environmental improvement; which is why Dupuis feels that its existence is not so paradoxical to one who loves the Camargue as it was. "We have to dream, but we cannot live off dreams," he says wistfully.

"I know the members of the Confrérie are ridiculed as the 'Brotherhood of Dreamers', but all I wish now is that I had written down my memories then. Now, I want to remember things that happened and I cannot. But it is strange, whenever I meet up with a friend of mine, who was also a *gardian*, though he now works as a customs officer in Port de Bouc, we spend hours talking about the past and about Baroncelli-Javon. When I knew the Marquis he was already very old, a small, wizened man, and very kind. He would leave a horse for me tied up at the station at Les-Saintes so that I could come down for a weekend, or the holidays, and ride straight out to find him." Dupuis has now taken over the job of archivist of the Confrérie and is collecting photographs and written souvenirs.

"We really were a brotherhood, too," he continues, bringing out the photographs and the old letters which he keeps in a file in his office. "I have the letters that passed between us telling us of arrangements, like this one: 'Mon cher ami ... I'm

Horse games in the arena at Arles

The trek to Le Cailar for summer pasture. *Gardians* at the time of Baroncelli-Javon

writing to say that the *ferrade* will be on . . . and there might be a horse for you.' That was from a *gardian*'s wife. Then from Baroncelli-Javon himself, I have a full correspondence, 'Mon cher André . . .', though we always wrote and talked in Provençal. It was a simple life and pure. We would ride all day, sleep rough at night, sometimes just on straw by the horse, worrying in case the horse moved about and kicked us in the face, and then continued the next day at three or four in the morning. We'd go from Les-Saintes to Nîmes, forty-five kilometres, in two days. Then there were the summer journeys to Le Cailar. This was before the Camargue itself was irrigated. Now there is really no need to take the bulls that far. Before, though, the grazing ground dried up in summer and disappeared in autumn under the rains. There is usually enough grazing ground now if the *manadiers* move the bulls round cleverly. Then, there would be two hundred or so beasts and *gardians* on horseback. It's the colours I remember most with the *gardians*' clothes and the sound of their voices shouting to the animals. Above all, we shared a love of the animals. It's a life that you could not find, or even dream of finding, today.

"Of course, it was Baroncelli-Javon who inspired most of that. When he first came to the Camargue, the *gardians* were a scruffy lot, and the beasts were very scraggy and were being sold off to the butchers. Baroncelli-Javon said a real *gardian* should wear the correct outfit and he made the rearing of bulls sacrosanct. He did so much for raising the national spirit that had become decadent. He even instilled in us that the costume to be worn had to be the right kind and not a cheapened variety. Even now, you can tell a real *gardian* by the cut of his trousers and the kind of material used.

"He did the same for the women too. Mistral had reinstituted the *Festo Virginenço*, but Baroncelli brought in the Queen of Arles competition every year. This is not like a beauty queen competition, for the girls have to be fluent in Provençal, be dignified, courteous, well-brought-up and be able to wear the Arlesienne costume with the grace intended. Angèle Vernet was the first Queen of Arles and Baroncelli rode with her, sidesaddle on the back of his horse, on the day of her wedding in 1936. Angèle is getting older now but she still upholds the Provençal traditions by working in Mistral's museum in Arles."

Dupuis had taken a break from his office job, pausing to gaze over the Camargue. Like many an ex-Camarguais, he still rides as an amateur *gardian* at weekends, on the land of his friend, the *manadier* Henri Laurent. "At the moment I'm riding to help the breaking-in of the horses. We train them very strictly to work with the bulls. You have to accustom them to the pull of the reins, so we have to do it a hundred times to be sure they'll turn quickly if necessary. If a bull is chasing you, you need to be able to get out of the way quickly. I got used to all that as a boy. At an *abrivade* or *course*, I'd be the one who had to ride in front of the bulls, galloping to the arena to get there first, open the gate and get out of the way just in time. I moved very fast in those days!"

It has been said that Baroncelli-Javon made aristocrats out of a lot of fading ranchers and farmers. He called them the *nouvelle aristocratie*, but the manners he introduced to this aristocracy were simply those of a particular country code. As Dupuis explains: "The *gardians* carry *tridents*, which are very sharp and you have to know how to use them or you can injure the animal. You would, for instance, never carry your own *trident* on to a *manade*. That is left for the *manadier* to offer you if he thinks you are experienced enough. To use it, you stab the bull, making him move in a certain direction and you use it under his tail when he has one back foot off the ground. To know when and how takes experience!"

Interest in the Camargue is not particularly widespread in France, apart from those who come from Paris to ride for the weekend and are annoyed to find they cannot go cantering off at will—living up to the Wild West image. When Baroncelli-Javon wrote the Preface to Baranger's little book, he said it brought tears to his eyes to read this document of their way of life that so few French people knew anything of. Similarly, Dupuis finds himself expressing surprise that anyone should ask him about his life in the Camargue (particularly an English person). He spreads the word through his own company, publishing articles on Camargue traditions in their magazine. He writes stories himself, in Provençal, and then has to translate them into French; and they are stories, like D'Arbaud's, that express the mystical quality of the Camargue. At the moment he is collecting stories from old Camarguais in the hope of bringing them together as *La Cabane aux Étangs* which might go some way to immortalising the memories.

He showed me one story, called *La Dame*. The action took place the night before Christmas when two horsemen were sitting quietly by the fire in a *cabane* in the middle of the Camargue, sheltering from the freezing night air. They heard a woman's cry and traced it to an *étang*. An oldish man and younger woman were stuck in the mud on the edge of the *étang*, on their way to Aigues-Mortes for the night. The two men helped them out, took them back to the *cabane* for the night and the next morning lent them clean clothes. They gave them a lift to Les-Saintes, where the young woman said she wanted to go and pray to the Marys for saving them and the baby that was about to be born. The two men sensed something strange. Later, their *gardian* brought back the clothes he had found left behind for them, and told them excitedly that when he had opened the package a light had shone out, like a star, and then flashed away. The story ends as the narrator says, "And I'm still wondering..." That's the kind of story, says André Dupuis, that most old Camarguais remember, part true stories, part dreams and part the mirage-like effect engendered by the Camargue's solitary wastes, where those who lived in solitude were left to the mercy of their imaginations.

## Chapter 11

## THE WINDS OF CHANGE

PEOPLE HAVE FEARED change in the Camargue since they first realised that the way of life in the delta was threatened. The whole of the Mistralian movement, followed so eagerly by Baroncelli-Javon and Joseph D'Arbaud, was an attempt to hold on to the past, but as the new century dawned the forces of change accelerated rapidly. It was time for something more dynamic than literary output. The idea of a national park to protect the area's wild nature had first been suggested by both Mistral and his apostle. That it was not formed then, not until half a century later, is most unfortunate, for by then it was a much weaker scheme. By then, the big changes had already happened. Through the centuries man had been chopping, destroying and laying waste; rooting out the trees, burning the land, overgrazing bulls, sheep and goats, and preventing the regeneration of land and vegetation. One of the earliest major effects on the whole of the south coast of France was, of course, tourism. It was the English aristocrats who first learned the pleasures of wintering and summering in warmer climes; and it is through the eyes of the area's earliest travellers that we can get a picture not only of the Camargue then, but of the way different generations perceived it and how they reacted to its all-too-obvious vulnerability.

One of the earliest visitors to the Camargue who recorded his impressions was Alexandre Dumas, who wrote up his journey of 1851 in *Pictures of Travel in the South of France*—a pleasant diversion and one of the first travel books. Dumas is interesting because he was visiting the south of France—Provence and the Camargue—before Mistral had appeared on the scene. What is remarkable is that he actually made it to the Camargue: very few outsiders would have been aware of, or attracted to, the area then. Dumas was not wildly impressed. He wrote:

> Here and there, in the midst of these putrid marshes of France, a poor habitation rises into view, where the hunter who is lost in these solitudes is sure of meeting with a morsel of bread and a little water; and of their bread and of that water, half is at the service of him who hungers and thirsts. . . . The Camargue uninhabited and uninhabitable as it is. . . .

That was not strictly true even in 1851 but may have been the beginnings of its "wild" image.

Yet, some little time earlier, Stendhal had also visited the Camargue and had written up his impressions in *Memories of a Tourist* in 1838. He said:

> The Camargue strongly resembles New Zealand: it forms an island, between the two branches of the Rhône and the sea; it is an equilateral triangle . . . the edges of this island are well cultivated, but sadly the middle is lower than the sides, and there you find *étangs*, salt marshes and fevers. The Étang de Vaccarès is the biggest of all. The vast uncultivated plains are covered with bulls and with sheep which roam freely.

Alphonse Daudet also wrote about the Camargue, having visited it as a direct response to Mistral. In his *Letters from my Windmill* (written to the north of the Camargue near Fontvieille), he describes the impressions of a young Parisian to the variety of Provençal life styles. His final section is on the Camargue. Daudet had gone there to hunt, but was moved by the place:

> Sinking our boats in the spongy soil, we find ourselves in wild Camargue. As far as the eye can reach are glittering

canals, pastures, fens and salt marshes ... no trees stand out to break the dreary monotony of the plain. ... As the sea is one unbroken vastness in spite of waves, so this plain is an unbroken vastness of desolation, heightened by the *mistral* in its remorseless, levelling career.

... I enjoy the salt breath from the marshes, the music of the reeds, the wind whispering through their long quivering stalks, the buzzing of innumerable insects. From time to time an eerie whirr sweeps through the air like the hollow murmur of the sea-shell. It is the cry of the bittern making for her fishing-ground. A flock of crane brush by, I hear the rustle of their wings, the fluttering of their down dishevelled by flight, almost the creaking of their jaded pinions. Then all is dark with just a glimmer of light in the water.

... There is neither church nor school in the neighbourhood and the malarious air of the Camargue is trying to children. Indeed, in summer, when the marshes are parched and the baked white ooze of the lakes cracks with the heat, the plain is unfit for human habitation.

But by the turn of the century, Mistral felt that things were on the move. The salt marshes no longer held out the ultimate threat of fever and malaria, the river had been dyked and embanked, rice had begun to be cultivated and the salt water was being replaced with vast quantities of river water. As Augustus John described his experience of returning to Martigues in the first quarter of the century in *Chiaroscuro*, so the same pressures were beginning to exert their weight on the Camargue: "... in submission to the march of progress, [it] was beginning to show more than one symptom of corruption: the air of peace and innocence which this little republic of fishermen used to wear was beginning to be overlaid by the blight of commerce".

On 26th May 1922, the Marquis de Baroncelli-Javon entertained assembled enthusiasts at the Mas de l'Amarée to a *ferrade* and *course* on the traditional feast day of the Marys, at Les-Saintes. The people there were from Provence and Languedoc, all members of Clubs Taurins from Bezier, Saint-

Gilles and Aigues-Mortes and people whom he knew shared his loves and his fears. Baroncelli-Javon delivered a memorable speech:

When the Master of Maillane was on the point of creating a museum, he hesitated a while between the idea of an ethnographic museum which he eventually formed in Arles, or an outdoor museum, to be a national park of the Camargue, where the pure races of bull and horse would be preserved, the flamingo, beaver and all the local fauna would be saved.

Having decided on the ethnographic museum in Arles, the Muséon Arlaten, Mistral said to me one day:

"I don't know the Camargue—the *gardians*, the bulls— well enough to create a park myself. But you, when the time comes, shouldn't miss out on it: it will be the complement to my Muséon."

Well, the moment has come to realise the Master's will. The Camargue more and more stands disfigured. The grazing grounds of bull and horse are becoming smaller daily. There is talk of drying Vaccarès. It's a miracle that we don't see factory chimneys pouring smoke over Les-Saintes-Maries.

The profession of the *gardian* has degenerated; since the war we hardly see any horse games. We seldom see bulls being led to the *courses* by horses. Instead wagons come right to the *manades* to take them away.

It's with difficulty that we have saved the last representatives of the races of bulls and horses and reconstituted the *manades*.

The time has certainly come for action, if we don't want our traditions to fade into nothingness. So, for that reason, we will set up a provisional committee to establish a park of the Camargue by public subscription.

We want Les-Saintes-Maries to continue to live encircled by an inviolable belt of mirages and virgin territory, where bulls and horses of the ancient races will always be raised, where reed cabins with their crosses will continue to defend us against invasions from the North. And we want the bulls and horses of this part to be used for *ferrades, abrivades* and *courses à cocardes,* in the purest of our traditions, in the town of Saintes, providing the Midi with its own national spirit.

If humanity today doesn't live for material preoccupations alone, then couldn't what exists in the Camargue be declared by the Government a National Park? We classify ancient stones, arenas, palaces, ramparts and cathedrals as historic monuments so no one can destroy them. Isn't Nature, at her most primitive and in the pure race of her animals, just as much a precious historical monument, which nevertheless could soon be destroyed by what we call civilisation?

Mistral had indeed formed an ethnographic museum in Arles, the Muséon Arlaten, generously using the cash he had received for his Nobel prize; the Muséon still stands as he created it. Baroncelli-Javon did not make a national park of the Camargue, though his efforts certainly ensured that it would be a viable project some thirty years later. Later, Elie Rull, a poet of the area, took up the cry about the disappearance of the pasture land and wrote a poem of protest against the proposed installation of a factory to lower the water level of Vaccarès so that the land could be used for agriculture. She dedicated her poem to Baroncelli-Javon.

> O Marquis, lorsque des machines
> Nous entendrons la respiration
> Ver les esclaves qui, dans l'usine
> Accomplissaient la profanation
> Tu lâcheras, à travers les friches
> Cent taureaux noirs, de tes plus farouches.

And the fears continued. By the 1940s, information about the Camargue was crossing the Channel, by way of English ornithologists and naturalists. In *Flamingo City,* the noted G. K. Yeates expressed his fears about the French government's threatened take-over of the Camargue as a military base, to be used for aircraft and exercise grounds. "The Camargue was recently threatened by the French War Office," he wrote. "That danger seems to have passed, only to have been replaced by an infinitely more serious menace. The cultivation of rice might at first sound innocuous . . . rice is very profitable and profit has attracted big capital. . . . Bulldozers rule where once the mosquito and wild bull held sway."

And it was rice that was really going to bring the changes.

# PART II

# CAMARGUE PRESENT

# Chapter 12

# THE WEALTH OF THE CAMARGUE

SOME PEOPLE CLAIM that the Camargue has never forgotten the riches and wealth it enjoyed during the splendid Roman epoch when the glamorous legionaries took up residence in villas on the isle. And despite the subsequent centuries of bleak subsistence farming, battling against wind and flood, the miserable way of life recorded by its early visitors and the overall gloomy aspect of the "grey wastes of dread", it was as if the Camargue was only biding its time until wealth came its way again. And so it did, at the end of the nineteenth century; and, quite naturally, through France's largest industry and first love—wine. At that time, phylloxera, a parasite that attacks the vine through its root, had destroyed the French vines twice and the wine growers were desperate to find some solution. The small area of viticulture in the Camargue remained unscathed. Some of these vines were planted in sand and others were probably exposed to larger quantities of water than found elsewhere on France's sun-kissed slopes. As a result it was discovered that, if the vine can be submerged in the autumn-winter period for forty or fifty days, the parasite is killed off. Large areas of the northern, more cultivatable parts of the Camargue were then planted with vines. The Camargue earned a lot of money—and a place in the history books. Phylloxera has been defeated by planting American vines now, but in the Camargue they still use the submersion method.

In the nineteenth century, however, agriculturalists in the Camargue were still anxious to find a reasonable method of submerging the soil for a lengthy period, as it was the only way of preparing the land for other forms of agriculture. The idea of rice had been toyed with for several centuries as a means of flushing the heavy salt content out of the soil. But, so far, despite many ingenious plans, no way had been found to pump water over the interminable flat land that did not entail a lot of expensive machinery. But, in the latter half of the nineteenth century, Étienne-Noel Godefroy emerged as the pioneer of rice culture. He was an inventive genius dedicated to improving farming. Up until then, the wry outlook among Camargue farmers had been that, far from being the pride of Provence and the wheat store for Gaul, the Camargue was the ruin of its proprietors and the grave of its cultivators.

Ever since the thirteenth century experiments had been noted and unsuccessfully copied; but in 1844 over a hundred acres of earth full of salt on one proprietor's land were levelled and irrigated. Godefroy had achieved an outstanding success, particularly as, at the time, no one had thought of monoculture. The Camargue was adaptable as it was made up of large properties whose owners could afford to give up vast tracts of land and share the costs.

The main enemy of rice cultivation has always been the diseases that breed in the marshes. Malaria was rightly feared. Godefroy himself died of the "marsh-fever" in 1847. But after Godefroy's experiment something else affected the Camargue that made the exploitation of rice vital. In 1858, the Rhône was embanked and the Camargue began to dry out. There was no natural control of the amount of salt in the earth as the river no longer flooded its banks. As the salt content increased, it began to permeate the northern, healthier parts, destroying the crops. It was an imperceptible process until, in the 1930s, the cry, "The Camargue is dying", was heard. The plan was then mooted to lower Vaccarès, and to drain and irrigate all the land. "Man had condemned the earth to a slow death by asphyxia, ruined his own livelihood by trying to protect it," it was said.

Up until 1936, there was a gradual increase in the amount of land being turned into rice paddies as the taste for rice had not been acquired in France. It was still mainly used as a cleaning process for more profitable crops such as wheat or lucerne. But in 1936 the bottom fell out of the rice market. Prices fell and farmers had to turn land back to traditional crops. Once more there were scarcely any paddy fields to be seen in the Camargue— despite the fact the delta had proved its suitability for rice growing.

Rice, therefore, is not only dependent on sun and water; like any other commodity it is equally subject to politics and economic forces. Its fluctuating history was once more re- written, this time by the War. When France lost Indochina and Madagascar, she also lost her cheap supply of what had, by then, become the new staple diet. In the immediate post-war period, vast acreage was again laid aside for rice and the mammoth task of levelling and irrigating was taken in hand by some of the huge machines through the Marshall Plan. Twelve thousand acres were again transformed. The new machinery meant less hard work and fewer labour problems. Machine sowing was introduced, using large tractors with steel wheels. The modern character of the Camargue was being shaped. It at once gained in exotic appeal but lost in interest for many of the purists and naturalists who loved the area. During the 1950s, there was a big expansion as rice became more popular; and the Camargue boasted that it supplied ninety per cent of France's domestic consumption. Of course, new chemicals and herbicides were being invented to help the process and, as it is said, "friends of the Camargue watched with fear". Some rice cultivists made a lot of money. Many of the properties turned over the majority of their land to the crop.

But the fluctuations have not finished yet, and rice is once again declining, forcing many farmers to turn their land thankfully back to the safer staples. Rice was never easy and was always fraught with danger. The largest acreage that could be planted with rice, forty thousand acres, has never been reached, and once again it is being planted in some areas simply as a means of "cleaning" the soil. But the Camargue has already been altered. The twenty-five thousand acres of paddy fields need up to forty thousand cubic metres of water a year. All this water is pumped from the Rhône into the paddy fields. In the 1950s it was then drained into Vaccarès where it was left to find its own way out. The result was the level of Vaccarès rose. Frightened residents began to talk about the need to drain Vaccarès straight into the sea to prevent flooding when the autumn rains came. The road to disaster for the delta could already have been taken. But by then Vaccarès was part of the Réserve de Camargue and no such action could be taken. Instead, in 1953, after a lot of arguing, the decision was taken to use the more costly and cumbersome method of pumping the Rhône water back into the Rhône, and now this is done by means of four main irrigation canals. That water has had rather more long-lasting effects, which we will see later.

## Chapter 13

# THE WHITE GOLD OF PROVENCE

SALT MAY HAVE been a burden to the agriculturalists of the Camargue, but another breed of farmer grew up over the years who was able to cash in on the crop itself: the crop that "grew" on the flat land by the sea, where the Mediterranean brine crystallises naturally under the heat of the sun and the force of the drying *mistral*. Prehistoric man appreciated the advantages of the salt he found there, and twentieth-century man and woman has certainly been able to exploit this resource to the full.

The mountains or *camelles* of salt, rising to fifty feet over the Camargue, may be the only high landmark for many miles. There are two main salt areas: Aigues-Mortes to the west of the Camargue and Salin-de-Giraud to the east. Both towns have factories for the cleaning and packing of salt, employing many hundreds of workers.

The naturally-formed salt flats (*salins*), shallow basins where sea water dries out, once formed an irregular patchwork beside the dunes, but exploitation has regularised the crazy-paving effect. By the thirteenth century, the money to be made from salt, and its diet value, had been realised and the Cistercian abbeys, notably the one of Psalmody, were bought out by Louis IX both for the salt and because he needed a stopping-off place on his journeys to the Crusades. The town of Aigues-Mortes developed from this and it was fortified by a large wall and two towers which remain today. But under Louis salt was also subject to a heavy tax and as it was harvested only once a year, there were often shortages. A healthy black market trade, smuggling it up the Rhône, was the natural result. It was not until the Revolution that salt was freed from such royal pleasure, and was taken over by the state; a law was made that there should be three harvests a year.

Salt was never easy to harvest as the *salins* covered such large areas. At Aigues-Mortes they stretch for fourteen kilometres and a canal is the only link with the hinterland. In earlier days, this meant that the working conditions were very remote, and the history of salt cultivation is not without its myths and legends. The workers were poor and isolated and there are stories of men who would stay out on the *salins* for months on end, their food being sent out by mule. The food was mainly *saucisson* and beans, which resisted the heat. But quarrels were so common about the pieces of *saucisson* that each man would mark his own piece before it went into the communal pot.

It was the severe floods of 1842 that first led to the amalgamation of the *salins*. Most were sold to a Monsieur Rigal who formed his own company. Others were privately owned, like the great Péchiney company which became the Salinière de Camargue. In 1850, the original parent company of the Salins du Midi was formed, finally to become the Salins du Midi and the Salins de l'Est. The town of Salin-de-Giraud was built at the same time, witnessing in its ugly growth the industrial revolution that made its existence necessary. Where once there had been a few *gardians*' and fishermen's *cabanes*, two factories appeared out of the mist and the working population was housed in tenements that would better fit a northern European mining town. The local railway was continued south from Arles to Les-Saintes and to Salin-de-Giraud to bring in workers and supplies, though the exit from the delta, across the Rhône at Salin, was never built and to this day the direct route across the river is by ferry, the Bac de Bacarin. In 1910, expressing quite contemporary-sounding fears, a local man wrote:

The Camargue, as with many other regions of France, has suffered these last few years from the influence of progress in all its forms, progress which has come from improvements brought in by communication links. The opening of the two railway lines, the construction of proper roads instead of the old tracks, while they ease agricultural sales, also give greater access to the visitor to the hidden corners of the delta.*

But the biggest jump in growth came with the Second World War. Until mechanisation, salt gathering was still difficult and local people continued to collect their own supplies by the ancient methods. One of the shrubs that grows in salty places is called *salsola*, a useful source of soda for washing and for glass manufacture. The leaves of the plant were collected, dried and cooked in oval shaped ovens, lined with silver, and roofed in pond-tortoise shell. The salt crystals were left round the sides of the oven.

By the twentieth century the amount of land being swallowed up by salt flats was quite staggering. Salin-de-Giraud increased tenfold the amount of land, developing a total of thirty thousand acres, while at Aigues-Mortes it was something over twenty thousand acres. The yield, although variable, can reach one million tons at Salin and about half that at Aigues-Mortes. The company of Salins du Midi is still relatively small. They produce wines, too, the Vins de Sable of Provence; vines planted in sand which, they proudly claim, contain no preservatives or chemicals. The company also rears and breeds bulls for the arena. The Salins company owns part of the pasturage in the *sansouire* and leases it to a *manadier* to rear Portuguese type bulls for the *corrida*. (Apart from that other Mediterranean local industry—Ricard, the pastis makers—where else is there an industrial company investing in bulls?)

The Salins du Midi is a powerful company in the area, owning land and being able to exert a wide influence on the affairs of the Camargue. They have drastically altered the appearance of the delta, giving a uniform pattern to a wild coastline and imposing the neat layout of dykes and roads, cutting up rectangular *salins* into solid rows, divided by pumping stations and wires. None of this, happily, has affected the

* D. G. Drouet: *Le Cheval Camargue.*

natural fauna—for wild birds love the *salins* and the Flamingoes, Avocets and Gulls make a secure home there among the salty flats. The company ensured this when they handed over the land for protection and created the nature reserve of the Camargue. For this favour, they have always enjoyed privileges in hunting the wild duck.

## Chapter 14

## THE FIRST PROTECTORS

WE CAN ONLY guess the reasons why the company, one day
to become the powerful Salins du Midi, handed over twenty-six
thousand acres to the care and protection of the SNd'AF in
1928. But if it was for the same reason that Péchiney and Salins
de l'Est had originally bought the central and southern parts of
the Camargue, it would be reason enough. In the first quarter of
the century, the salt industrialists feared that the fresh water
brought in for rice growing, building up in the Étang de Vaccarès,
would unbalance the water system of the delta and pose a potential
threat to the *salins*. Perhaps they thought that if they put the land
under the management of the voluntary society of naturalists,
the wild life would be preserved and the environment would be
stabilised as a result.

In those early days of awareness to nature, societies such as
the SNd'AF were not so much interested in conservation as in
observation of nature. No one talked then in terms of threats.
But they were interested in maintaining a peaceful environment
for the bird-life of the Camargue and in ensuring that genuine
ornithologists and naturalists would have access to the territory.
It was the peaceful fecundity of wild life which also interested
the salt companies who were then, and still are, talented and
passionate hunters. There was no idea then of regulating
hunting.

Originally, the land was leased for forty years. In 1960, the
SNd'AF became associated with the Société Nationale de
Protection de Nature (SNPN) which had been founded in 1901
by the Natural History Museum in Paris. The full society,

blessed with the name Société Nationale de Protection de Nature et d'Acclimatation de France, probably carried less weight than its impressive title; but it has always been active in the field of conservation, and under its present president, François Bourlière, achieves international recognition for its work in ecology. It produces the monthly journal *La Terre et La Vie* and the *Courrier de la Nature*. Writing in a 1930s issue of *La Terre et La Vie*, on why France needed national reserves and parks, a naturalist pointed out that in this, France lagged behind the rest of the world: America, Sweden, Belgium and even Britain were already busy creating their own nature reserves. The gift from the salt companies put the SNPNd'AF on an international footing. The Camargue was to become its first nature reserve to be protected from the ravages of the future. And, surprisingly, the amount of control exerted over the land was quite severe. It is one of the reasons why the Camargue is as safe and sound as it is today. Contemporary regulations dare not be so severe on humanity and tend to be harsher on nature.

The aim of the Réserve Zoologique et Botanique de Camargue was to close off its grounds to casual visitors; to forbid the taking away of any plant, bird, or material for any use and to encourage visits from serious students or bird-watchers who were first required to visit the Réserve's office to obtain permission and be offered the help of a guard if necessary. The presidents of the Réserve have always been strong local figures, like Gabriel Tallon and the *Grand Caff*, M. de Caffarelli, a pensioner who, until recently, was the outspoken and well-known caretaker for the Réserve, working from a crumbling old Provençal house in the back streets of Arles (the rue Honoré-Nicholas that many a British ornithologist must have visited: the British are well respected as bird-watchers).

In its early days the Réserve made sure that the land was no longer used to graze bulls and horses, was not trampled on by humans and that the bird life was not disturbed. But despite its severity, it developed an eccentric relationship with the people of the Camargue.

The story of this relationship was told to me by René

Charavin, the current lively young director of the Réserve. The area it covers takes in the whole central part of the Camargue; which is why it is safe to say that no casual visitor can ever really know the delta: there is so much land he can never see. But the Réserve's boundaries are still subject to ancient agreements, rights and traditions. To the north-east, for instance, is one of the four houses used by the Réserve. Because of an oversight, this house is still owned by the Salins du Midi, so the rules against hunting there cannot hold. Then the significance of the "no hunting or fishing" rule for the Étang de Vaccarès was somewhat weakened by the fact that almost a third of its surface is still owned by private proprietors, such as the huge Mas de Méjanes owned by Ricard, who still hold the fishing rights. Again, there is the lovely Île de Mornes, just to the south-west of Vaccarès, which is now state-owned, but the family retains the right to cross it and hunt on it. The Digue de la Mer, constructed by the commune of Les-Saintes-Maries in 1861, is still owned by them and so, between the beach and the Digue, the Réserve is at its most vulnerable. On Amphise, the Mas le Paradis still belongs to an eccentric farmer, M. Pourquier, who has hung on to old property rights which run out this year—so, as he is a breeder of the Portuguese strain of bulls, there are actually bulls grazing on the Réserve. The massive stretch of land which makes up the Mas Fiélouse and the Étang du Fournelet, is also private property and the Réserve has no right to cross the land—although it is adjacent to the state-owned territory.

However, for all its problems, the Réserve is relatively free from outside pressure. Its most immediate neighbours are the private reserve of the Tour du Valat and the public one of Les Impériaux. All these complex patterns of ownership are typical of the Camargue, for what is in question there all the time is the balance between people and nature.

In 1961, the Salins du Midi company changed its set-up and decided to regulate the future of the Réserve. They made a contract with the government for seventy-five years, which meant the SNPNd'AF could plan ahead till 2036. Then, in 1972, the final change was made. Conservation by then having become a political as well as ideological issue, the Réserve of the Camargue was becoming too important in the eyes of the world to be left to the whim of salt industrialists. The state was involved in complicated dealings to acquire the land it needed for industrial development to the east of the Camargue, and the Réserve lands were sold to the Ministry of the Environment for a nominal one franc, and in return the salt company gained some more land for *salins*. The Réserve also received another seven thousand acres. The World Wildlife Fund had made this possible by a gift of five million francs.

Since 1973, the Réserve has had two new directors appointed and a new rôle devised. It still welcomes over a thousand visitors and researchers a year and about five hundred groups who want to be shown around: but public relations and niceties are not its prime function. The Réserve can now act as the focal point for a wide variety of research and controlled studies carried out by various bodies. It is impossible, they point out, to study everything in the Réserve, but what they are hoping to do is to find out what types of evolution are taking place and what controls, if any, are needed. They now have a direct line to the Ministry of the Environment.

The Réserve wants to reflect the world-wide consciousness, and hopes that visitors to the Camargue come to understand why the flora and fauna are indigenous to the area and not merely to stand and stare. They are busy preparing maps that point out the location of types of vegetation and wild life; while at the same time trying to discourage some of the hundreds of amateur bird-watchers, film-makers and photographers in general who come just so they can say they've been. On the other hand, René Charavin knows that they will have to extend their hand in one other new direction, that is towards the farmers and inhabitants of the Camargue who may themselves long to visit the Bois des Rièges but have not yet the chance to see this focal point of their own folklore.

The move towards research and more intensive ecological

*Gardian*, with *trident*, rides his horse through an *étang* as evening falls

The funeral of Baroncelli-Javon in 1943

The salt *camelle* at Salin-de-Giraud

study can be attributed to the work of one man, Luc Hoffmann, who certainly made the optimum use of a paradoxical source of wealth. When Hoffmann bought the *mas*, the Tour du Valat, from a Marseilles businessman, he had no thoughts of potential dangers or threats that would soon be widespread, but he did want to study the flora and fauna of this fascinating wetland. His first move was to set up a ringing station so that the routes of the Camargue's visiting bird-life could be traced. The work of the station boomed and he now has an international staff of Swiss, British, German and French; an assistant director, Bettina Goldschmidt-Rothschild (from another formidable European family), and a fluctuating group of students and assistants who spend the summer at the *mas*. Most of the employees live on the premises turning it into a mini-United Nations.

Although they are now changing the scope of their work into broader based ecological studies, Hoffmann is aware that even as a ringing station they were, for long years, the only people actively involved in protecting the Camargue from the marauders of the twentieth century. Something of a lone campaigner, from the beginning he wanted to widen his studies from birds to the whole complex of the region: to study the co-existence of every living organism within it. He sought the help of the French government but with no avail, and he had to content himself with a purely ornithological programme using keen amateurs. Even so, they soon became the largest bird-ringing station in Europe. But it was during those early years that Hoffman's interest was broadened as he witnessed the threat to the natural equilibrium brought about by rice cultivation and intensive farming. He became aware then of the vulnerable balance of the area and the dangers threatening it. A catalyst for him was the 1958 conference of IUCN (International Union for Conservation of Nature and Natural Resources), in Athens, which he attended as a visitor and was, he says, his first active participation in the world of conservation.

From then on Hoffmann became increasingly involved in conservation issues and was interested in co-ordinating information on marshlands. At the next conference, two years later, he was made "Co-ordinator of Project MAR". In 1961, he became Honorary Director of the International Wildfowl Research Bureau, a post he held for seven years. Meanwhile he also became president of the IUCN, and is still involved with them. During this period, in the early 60s, he widened his sights to the Coto Donana, in Spain, where there was another tract of marshland which, unless it was bought quickly, would soon fall into the hands of the developers. He raised funds independently, and within a few months had enough to save the area. Then, in Britain, a group of prestigious conservationists was establishing a foundation, on an international basis, for raising money (for projects such as the one in Spain) and when the World Wildlife Fund was formed, with Prince Bernhard and Peter Scott as president and vice-president, Luc Hoffmann was made second vice-president, and now he is executive vice-president, and president of the IBRS (International Bureau of Research into the Sauvagine), responsible for humid zones in the Mediterranean. He is also on the administrative council of the SNPNd'AF and, closer to home, leads the fight for conservation of the Camargue.

From the mid-50s, he received help from scientists at the Centre Nationale de Recherche Scientifique, in nearby university centres; and from 1970, he saw the kind of help he wanted when the CNRS built a laboratory right at his door. The Centre d'Écologie de la Camargue, Tour du Valat, and the Réserve all now work in co-operation, though in very different ways, in an effort to find just what is the ecological make-up of the Camargue—before it is too late.

They know the Camargue is changing, and that collecting data is no longer sufficient. There is the problem of endangered species and fast changing zones. They are now attempting a detailed study of the area: studies of freshwater marshes, brackish lakes, and saltwater vegetation are all as important as knowing which birds breed and feed where. It is not a question of being able to study every blade of grass in the Camargue, but of selecting the important species or families to study. The time has gone for cries of delight at the beauty of nature; what is needed now is understanding and awareness. If the Camargue is to change and if that is uncontrollable, then they want to know what it was that made it so unique. At least our descendants should be left with that information—if they cannot have the genuine article.

When Luc Hoffmann first came to the Camargue in the 50s, naturalists did not worry about politics and the reverse was even more true. But, by the mid 50s, things were changing; the effects of land reclamation for agriculture and heavy irrigation for rice had altered the face of the Camargue, and no one knew what had been done to its soul. Hoffmann wrote *An Ecological Sketch of the Camargue* in which he noted what changes he could already see. It was no alarmist document, just careful observation, though he did end on a warning note: "The Camargue is a landscape undergoing profound trans-formation and its protectors have a heavy responsibility."

What had happened was that the twenty-five thousand acres of land put under water for rice were taking between twenty and forty thousand cubic metres of water per acre, per year, and the vast acreage of vines was also consuming yet more water—altogether the volume was anything up to four hundred million cubic metres of water a year. (That is today's figure; there was a steady increase from the 1950s.) It was in the 1950s that the great period of desalination began. This process was so rapid that, in 1955, a plan had to be devised to evacuate some of that extra water as there was a danger of flooding. The water was then pumped back into the Rhône (all except some fifty million cubic metres which still go into Vaccarès). But that is not the end of the story. In the 1950s, the Rhône was relatively clean; but that is no longer the case, and it is now the polluted water from the Rhône, leaving its deposits in the earth and finally in Vaccarès itself, which causes most concern. The menace of hydrocarbons, chemicals and industrial waste products in the Rhône is added to by that of the herbicides and insecticides used quite liberally in rice production. It is in these

areas that ecological studies are being made. They are not a
cure, but a study of the symptoms.

In 1958, Luc Hoffmann first outlined the effects of the
changing water levels. He pointed out that visitors still naïvely
thought the Camargue was a land of virgin soil; but that in
reality it had been changing as a result of human intervention
for the past two centuries. The kinds of change are not
spectacular to the untrained eye but they are extremely
significant. Because what happens, in an area as vulnerable as
the Camargue, is that different types of wild life are attracted
to the area and become dominant over the original species.
The habitat that made the Camargue unique was beginning
to disappear before his eyes.

To describe best what he actually observed, I will draw on
Hoffmann's findings in his *Ecological Sketch*. The effects on the
bird populations of using the land for rice and other farming
could be seen in three categories. There were the species of
birds which probably only colonised the Camargue as a
consequence of this reclamation; the ordinary species of the
natural Camargue able to take advantage of habitats created by
cultivation; and the species that were actually reduced by
agricultural reclamation. He emphasised that these were his
observations and that theories cannot be supported simply
because of them. For example, the species attracted to the
Camargue as a result of more sophisticated growth of crops
include: Lesser Kestrel, Quail, Woodpigeon, Great Spotted
Cuckoo, Barn Owl, Little Owl, Tawny Owl, Swift, Crested
Lark, Woodlark, Swallow, House Martin, Carrion Crow,
Jackdaw, Orphean Warbler and Lesser Grey Shrike. Of those
that were present in the Camargue anyway but had benefited
from the crops, or may just have switched their usual habitat,
there were: Purple Heron, Little Egret, Squacco Heron, Night
Heron, Mallard, Teal, Garganey, Black-tailed Godwit, Wood
Sandpiper, Black-winged Stilt, Herring Gull, Black-headed
Gull, Black Tern, Whiskered Tern, Gull-billed Tern, Golden
Oriole, Magpie, Great Tit, Nightingale, Melodious Warbler,
Blackcap, Linnet and Corn Bunting. In the third group, there

seem to be considerably fewer species reduced by rice cultivation. But since these are generally the species which are characteristic of the *wild* Camargue and less common elsewhere in Europe, the decline in numbers is of considerable significance. For the ecologist it is an undesirable type of evolution, as it means that the Camargue can offer less information on bird populations. The rarer birds are giving way to more adaptable and more common ones—a process which is causing very great concern. The French have a nice word for the process; they call it *banaliser* which should translate literally as "to banalise", and although we don't have a word like that, the meaning is clear enough.

In the 1950s the endangered, or diminishing, species were Red-legged Partridge, Lapwing, Stone Curlew, Pratincole, Pin-tailed Sandgrouse, Roller, Short-toed Lark, Skylark, Tawny Pipit, Yellow Wagtail, and Great Grey Shrike. But since then, the list has grown or changed. Ecologists will not sensationalise their findings: it is difficult to theorise until several years later. And, then, some changes are caused by man, some by climate, and some by other predatory animals. It is easy these days to blame ourselves, although some would say that all these changes must be indirectly due to man. For example, though, there are causes such as the ones noted by G. K. Yeates. He said that in 1938 "after only one winter without rain, the transformation was impressive"; in 1947, during an extremely cold winter, when Arles had been under snow for six weeks, birds such as the Egret were used for food. "The inside of a human stomach," he wrote, "seems a sad end for a Little Egret or Night Heron." More recently, the reduced numbers of some species arriving in the Camargue could very well have been caused by the famine in the Sahel desert of Africa, when many more would have been shot for food.

Nevertheless, by the late 50s, people in the Camargue had begun to take their responsibilities seriously, and the Réserve was awarded a Council of Europe conservation diploma in 1965 as an area where protection was to be encouraged. By the 60s, though, that other great disturber of the peace had arrived:

F

the tourist. Ornithologists and conservationists both realised that they could not jealously guard the treasures of the Camargue for themselves; that nature, and particularly wild nature, had to be open to the public starved, as they were, of natural beauty in their overcrowded cities. The Camarguais were working towards creating some kind of Park, through which they could order and channel the preservation and tourism of the delta—at the same time hoping to keep it under their own control. Hoffmann was about to play a great role as an ornithologist, a conservationist and as a lover of the Camargue. He was already a much respected, though shadowy, figure locally—but he had an unsuspected sympathy for the needs of the tourist and realised that areas like the Camargue should be made available as leisure centres. He argued thus:

This is not only the biggest untouched area which exists in France (outside of some mountain districts which are of a poorer nature), it is also probably the most varied, and bio-logically the richest in Western Europe. One has known for several years, that saltwater areas are among the most productive of natural habitats. And the Camargue has the largest expanse of saltwater in Europe. This shows itself in the richness of its fauna, its invertebrate animals and its birds. We've seen that it represents an irreplaceable bridgehead, resting place and winter feeding grounds. If it disappeared, there would be unforeseeable consequences for the winged creatures of many European countries. . . .

If the international and national value of the Camargue is a powerful justification for its conservation, there are others which, on a regional scale, are just as important.

It would be unjust that all this wild beauty, and primitive life, should remain a hunting ground for researchers only. A large public, inhabitants and tourists alike, should also be able to profit.

Yet it is obvious that so many perspectives can't come under the umbrella of one organisation, the present Réserve of the Camargue. On one hand, it is necessary to protect vast areas as peace havens for fauna and flora, but on the other hand, nature trails, horse rides and motoring tours need organising: as do hunting-grounds and fishing areas to enable the public to enjoy the full extent of its riches.*

To many, it seemed as if the death knell had already tolled. The "banalisation" of the Camargue as a tourists' nature reserve, with horse-rides and nature trails mapped out for the slothful city person (one imagines something like Yosemite National Park in California which, on crowded summer days, can be almost Disneyesque), was becoming too real a fear. Nevertheless, it was eight years before a Park was created under one charter by the Camarguais, who were trying, first and foremost, to protect themselves and to rationalise all the different interests. The quarrels about how best to achieve this have not stopped yet.

* Luc Hoffmann and Jacques Blondel: *L'Originalité et le Rôle de la Camargue.*

## Chapter 15

## WINTERING DUCKS AND
## SUMMERING TOURISTS

---

THE CAMARGUE, TINY area that it is, is under great pressure
and not only from problems within itself. It was finally the
outside pressures, so visible to any eye, that led to the formation
of a park. There seem to be four major pressures exerting their
individual forces on the nature reserve and threatening to
destroy the unique way of life of the delta. They are: the hunting
of wild duck; the increasing numbers of tourists; the building of
six new resorts along the coast from Aigues-Mortes to Perpignan,
with the consequent threat of a similar land-grab in the delta,
and the pollution that may have come from killing the
mosquitoes there; and, finally, the pollution crisis brought on
by the growth of Fos-sur-Mer into the second largest port in
Europe, and its hinterland into a huge industrial belt. Fos
is but fifteen miles to the east of the Camargue and its mush-
rooming oil refineries have become a concrete threat on the
Camargue's horizon. Port Camargue, one of the new resorts, is
literally at the delta's west side door, just to the south of Aigues-
Mortes. In both cases, the expanse of marshes has been seen as
a wasteland which has not been put to an economic use.
Who knew if the Camargue wouldn't one day be seen to be
more useful as a new airport, or for a super new highway, for
building, or for storing oil? It is not surprising the people on
this island should have felt some shivers of fear.

By the time a Camarguais could go down to the sea's edge,
by the Étang de Fangassier, to look with wonder at the
Flamingoes and find his eyes caught, not by the pink flash of a

wing, but by the violent red of an industrial tower rising out of the horizon; by the time he could travel through the Petite Camargue towards the ancient fortress of Aigues-Mortes and watch the concrete blocks of holiday flats rising out of the marshes; only then were the warning signs loud and clear. But the hybrid assortment of residents of the delta, and their varying interests, meant that action against these threats came too slowly and too late. To the north of the delta, in the mountainous region of the Alpilles, there were similar threats from housing development as plot after plot of land was sold off for holiday villas. There, a league for the defence of the Alpilles was set up, slogans were plastered on walls and angry meetings were held in local towns halls. The Camarguais, being insular and independent by nature, did not unite in the same way. But more of that in the next chapter.

Marshland, saline lagoon, scrub land and salty water meant, to the east and west of the delta, that the land had been left more or less untouched. It had never been easy to build on, or to cultivate. The south coast of France, so affluent along the Côte d'Azur and so busy at the old port of Marseilles, had been left to fend for itself in its less productive stretches. There is a length of over one hundred miles, between Aigues-Mortes and Perpignan, which has idled its way into the twentieth century. It was populated with fishing villages, one of the largest of which was Sète (which still boasts some of the best sea food restaurants) and was discovered only by the few tourists who liked deserted beaches. But under de Gaulle growth was encouraged and France, feeling that it was being left behind in the race for industrial and commercial wealth, began to use these vacant stretches of land. In 1961 the French government set out to achieve in ten years what had taken a century to create on the Riviera. The coastline of Languedoc-Roussillon was to be developed to attract middle-class French tourists and distract them from the rush to Spain: in resorts such as Port Camargue, Grande-Motte, Carnon, Port-Leucate, Port-Barcarès and Cap d'Agde.

The growth of these new resorts has become immortalised in

a new phrase in the language: *la grande motte* is now used by travellers who take one look at a fishing village and find that it has turned into a commercial resort overnight. For Grande Motte is the largest, most advanced and perhaps most controversial of any of the new resorts. They were all conceived and managed by Pierre Racine of L'École Nationale d'Administration—a formidable nursery for technocrats in Paris. To be irresistible to a futuristic concept of the holiday-maker, each new resort was designed by one chief architect. The architect of Grande Motte was Jean Balladur, who planned the creation around Egyptian-style pyramids, honeycombing holiday apartments each with balcony and guaranteed sunshine, stacked one upon the other—just like the city apartment blocks most of the holiday-makers would have been escaping from. The town also has a "brave new world" system of electric cars and pedestrian areas but, like so many concrete wildernesses, it has as much soul as you find on a wet afternoon in a holiday camp. Commercially it has been a success. And each year the numbers arriving increase, bringing with them their cars and their boats. For these new resorts were made not only to house half a million people for three months of the year, but also to take forty thousand pleasure boats. They were aimed directly at the new bourgeoisie of France's consumer society: the young and temporarily affluent who wanted to invest in holiday property.

All this was only possible with a five-year investment plan of eighty million pounds, and with the confidence that it could work. Echoing the poet Mistral, General de Gaulle said in 1967, "I find the scheme grandiose, but perfectly feasible". And it was Philippe Lamour, of the Cie d'Aménagement de Bas-Rhône-Languedoc, the drainage station near the Camargue, who perhaps helped create the confidence. Having already brought water to the nearby farming areas, he was able to ensure that sufficient drinking water could be brought to these new towns.

It was the mosquitoes in the marshes that had been responsible for keeping the tourists at bay. Those who visit the

Camargue are perhaps already prepared to suffer for the sake of the natural life but, to entice thousands of sun-seekers to the area, the mosquito problem first had to be eliminated. This was a mammoth task and one that shows how determined the French government was to make a success of the scheme.

Attacking the mosquitoes was a matter of war and the agencies involved had to deploy their best and most expensive tactics. This part of the whole venture alone cost seven million pounds in insecticides. Six thousand breeding sites were identified and sprayed selectively with phosphorous liquids from helicopters. The spraying was carried out when the larvae were hatching and then the weed-beds were cleared. The mosquito did not have a chance against the combined forces. The area was cleared and was then ready to be built on. New road systems, a motorway, drainage, electricity and, finally, housing began to rise out of the once flat wasteland. An example of the kind of euphoria that such massive development produced in those days is found in typical reportage of the scheme, this one is from a British paper: ". . . it is a good way to invest public and private money and one which had already made a major impact on the fauna, flora, topography and economy of the little-known area and hitherto uneconomic Languedoc-Roussillon coast."

Did the journalist write that with irony or naïvety? The flora and fauna had already been radically altered. When insecticides are sprayed to kill mosquitoes, the cycle of destruction spreads to the birds who also feed in the same weed-beds and eventually to humans themselves. How much of the insecticides was carried, by the wind, to the more important territory of the nature reserve of the Camargue where the mosquitoes have not been destroyed? The prevailing wind is the north-westerly *mistral*, which should take most of the effluent straight out to sea, but there are also strong westerlies. Worse still, the marshlands of the coastal strip, called wastelands by modern man because they were uneconomical, were home to wild duck and other aquatic species, just as is the delta itself.

So the total area of breeding grounds has been drastically reduced.

The coastline has been developed from the Côte d'Azur to Languedoc-Roussillon, with the Camargue lying uncomfortably between the two. To the east of the delta, just fifteen miles from the course of the Grand Rhône, and thirty miles west of the great port of Marseilles, lies the new industrial and port complex of Fos-sur-Mer. It will be more than interesting to see what becomes of this new industrial block, built simultaneously with the growing awareness of environmental protection. Some forty thousand acres have been zoned for Fos's growth, along the coast and tracing back up the course of the Rhône (though there is a belt of land by the Rhône itself which is protected from any of the heavy industries).

Fos is being developed to increase the amount of trade coming to the south, which was previously shunned by anything other than Mediterranean or colonial traffic. The landspace used will be equal to the size of Paris and the trade is expected to be equal to that of Rotterdam. The area has already attracted a great number of heavy industries: the steel works of Wendel-Sidelor, now called Solmer, and the chemical industries of ICI; some of the major production will be in oil refining, expanding that already situated round the Étang de Berre—Esso is at Fos itself, Shell at Berre, BP at Lavera and Total-SCF at La Medo. Optimists and some economists already presume that the present development of Fos is carrying on the traditions established by the Greeks in the sixth century BC, when Fossae Maritimae was built up as a port and then expanded by the Romans who constructed a canal from Fos into the hinterland. The old fishing village still remains atop the only hill in the area. To see the dismal picture of what the growth of Fos into the second largest port in Europe might actually mean, the visitor has only to drive towards the scene.

Thankfully the Camargue is separated from the Marseilles conurbations by the Grand Rhône and joined by a ferry boat which leaves every twenty minutes for its five-minute glide across the river; in its own anachronistic way this discourages heavy transport and much traffic from going into the Camargue. It is an interesting ride, as the Rhône is wide and majestic at that point. Once you have crossed, there is the town of Port St Louis at your feet. Port St Louis retains some charm and is still a small industrial concern. But the road that then leads to Marseilles traverses a real twentieth-century wasteland.

The area near and around Fos was made up of marshes, lagoons, and infertile ground. It is flat and grey from alluvial mud. Now industry has suffocated the area like a shroud. Large cooling towers, huge blocks of factories, chimneys burning off chemical gases, and petrol refineries, emerge out of the industrial fog like giant bogymen. There is nothing to break up the ugly landscape. Just the endless trail of lorries transporting the goods to a communications point: lorries that appear as if suspended above the land level, running on mini-train lines, along set tracks, incongruously across a desert of mud and water.

This was once home to the bird life of the marshes. It was bought at very low prices by a government whose intentions were not then revealed. The marshes were drained and pre-pared. As one horrified eye-witness noted, straw was laid on top, and, once the marshes had dried up, huge clouds of dust, blown by the *mistral*, would hover over the desert. As the land settled, it was built on. There are still birds in the area, of course. You can see Swallows, House Martins, Swifts and Gulls, hunting desperately for their old feeding grounds. But how they survive the smells coming from the industrial gases and chemical outpourings is as much a mystery as how the humans living there survive. A thick, yellowish pall of industrial smog hangs over the area. The itching smell fills the throat and the soul. And, just as pathetic as the birds, are the migrant workers, housed on temporary caravan sites and in mobile homes.

Fos was a big issue during the presidential election which brought in Giscard d'Estaing. Standing on the environmental ticket, René Dumont visited Fos and said he would promise

improvements. But, to some, Fos is already a white elephant
and so doomed to failure. Its projected one million population
by 1980, already around a quarter that size, is proving to be a
problem. Will the nearby towns be developed as dormitory
towns for the workers? In fact, will Fos hang like a dead weight
on the area, providing no extra employment for the already
severely under-employed south, but merely bring in temporary
skilled workers from the outside who will stay only while the
work lasts? Will the heavy industries choke the remaining
lagoons and kill off for ever the area's indigenous trade—
fishing? Local meetings have accused the government of selling
out to big industry, when the area could have been better
served with more light industries which, in turn, would have
employed existing residents. And then what about pollution?
The thick yellow cloud can escape no one's notice, and
one can only pity the residents of the ancient village of
Fos-sur-Mer.

The Camarguais have been watching the situation carefully
during the two years since Fos was built. Pollution testers are
set up for air and water, and are placed on farming land in the
Camargue—though most local opinion feels that the *mistral*
will be their saviour, blowing the gases and pollutants out into
the sea. While complacency abounds over the threat to themselves, what actually *did* happen at the Étang de Berre is not
forgotten. The Étang was once the centre of a flourishing fishing
industry, but now most of the shellfish are dead, and only eels
remain. The Étang, as I have said, has been used by petrol
companies for many years, with the result that it is now, in
effect, dead, and mercury traces have been found in any fish
that still survive. But it is not only the *étangs* that are at risk.
As one local ecologist said, they have put petrol refineries on the
shores of an enclosed sea, the Mediterranean, and it would only
need one accident—an explosion or leakage—for the whole of
that sea to be destroyed.

Local scientists, ecologists and marine biologists have been
saying for some years that the Mediterranean has become a
dustbin, although, in fact, the question of pollution has never

been overlooked. Anti-pollution measures take up between five and ten per cent of the total cost of building factories or refineries. All water is cleaned and recycled, and it is forbidden to deposit any waste into either the river or the sea. From the beginning, the government set up a society to protect the area, the SPPI (Permanent Secretariat against Industrial Pollution). It is controlled by the Government and not by a regional body. Its critics say this is why it is so ineffective: so far it has issued some one hundred and twenty-two reports but has inaugurated no new measures. The major industries at Fos, showing their willingness to take responsibility for the pollution problems, also organised themselves into an association (AIRFOBEP), aiming to study the effects and take curative measures. As is often pointed out, though, these type of measures are never taken until something has been spotted—by which time it is often too late.

The Camargue is also under pressure from within the delta's own limits. One of its paradoxes is that, although it is one of the largest and most important nature reserves in western Europe, it is also a significant area for hunting. The economy of the delta relies on hunting; and, surprisingly, so does the natural state of large areas of the *sansouire*. Had hunting not been an economically viable way of using the land, it would not have been left in such a wild state. Most of the big proprietors, rice cultivators, salt farmers and ranchers own land which they keep for hunting. This *réserve de chasse* is the land which attracts the duck populations. Many people, therefore, take the view that hunting is a lesser evil than artificial cultivation which would deter the ducks from coming at all. About a hundred thousand ducks are shot each year and no one yet knows whether they can survive that rate of depletion, though Luc Hoffmann, for example, feels that the pressure from hunting is not yet so high that it has reached the level of over-shooting.

The moral question of hunting is another issue, and ecologists and ornithologists seem to have reached a compromise over it. To the visitor, though, it can be an upsetting experience. From August to March the Camargue can seem like a battlefield, the anti-hunters say. Bullets fly around the roads and police and Réserve guards have to patrol them to stop illegal shooting and make sure no barrels are pointed in the direction of the Réserve or Tour du Valat land. The hunting season opens on 15th August. It continues until the first Sunday in January for most birds and game, and until 31st March for water birds.

There are some two thousand official huntsmen who pay the magnificent sum of twenty thousand francs (around two thousand pounds), to shoot for one season and who take part in what some call a massacre, killing every bird they see and selling their victims to the *gibier* (fowl butcher), to recoup some of their investment. Another ten thousand amateur hunters from Arles and the other nearby cities come to the Camargue for weekends and on days off. They are the *chasse communale* who have no legal right to hunt, but line the sides of the roads and take pot shots. The same number of ducks return every year, and as long as the figures do not drop, there is no immediate cause for concern.

The annual passage begins in early July, when the waders first come in. There are some twenty-five species and they continue to arrive for five months; the first flocks come when the marshes are drying up during the summer heat, and so there is a greater concentration of little water-borne invertebrates for the birds to feed on. Around two hundred thousand ducks stay for the whole winter, and the sight of them can be awe-inspiring. They breed and feed, resting on the marshes, and go into the Réserve for their food.

The migration of numerous species of smaller birds is less spectacular, but, over four months, eighty species arrive, stay for four of five days, fill up with food, and then set off again on their long transcontinental flight. The effect of these invasions on the Camargue is something that is constantly being watched. How can the vegetation cope? How is it that for half a year it can offer food and living space to a minimal population, and for the next half to such a large crowd? It is one of the less known wonders of the world.

It is their feeding and breeding habits which lead to the ducks' downfall. For the birds rest peacefully during the day, and at night hunt for food. It is when they fly from the *étangs* to the marshes, at dusk, that they are caught by the shot; also, many ducks die from lead poisoning as they pick up pellets or shot as they hunt for grit in the Camargue's stoneless ground. The rings taken from the ducks that are shot, and returned to the ringing station, show how many birds are crippled or maimed by the hunters. Yet, in many cases, the ducks become wise to their predators. At the beginning of a season, many an ornithologist will tell you, the birds fly low and are caught. By the middle of the season they fly that much higher.

There are three kinds of duck shoot in the Camargue: the *passée*, *affût* and *battue*. The *passée* is the lot of the *chasse communale* who wait on the roads under the flight routes at dusk when the birds go for food. They do not shoot very many. The *affût* is the game of the sportsman who hides by a sheet of water at dusk or dawn and fires as the ducks try to land. Their chances are not too high either, though the duck is approaching at an easier angle. It is the *battue* which really angers conservationists. The *battue* only takes place four or five times a year, when those huntsmen who can afford to pay gather round a *remise* before sunrise; the ducks are frightened and in the crude and ostentatious massacre that follows some three to five hundred ducks may be killed in one hour.

For three consecutive winters, from 1969–72, there was a fear of over-shooting as numbers seemed to be declining. But, from 1972–4, the numbers increased to 1969 levels. It is essential to continue the counts and to keep a sharp eye on an increase in numbers of huntsmen; and to report these findings to the hunting regulators in Paris. If over-shooting became a reality, then some measure of control would have to be taken. In the meantime, as conservationists often number among the most ardent hunters, not much is likely to happen. And one can ask what would happen to the Camargue if the hunting of wild duck suddenly stopped? There might be just as great a massacre from lack of food and space. Hunting has become a part of the natural balance, and cannot be ignored.

Tourism also has its economic benefits and its environmental drawbacks. Up to the early 1950s, the Camarguais point out, there were hardly any tourists. For the last ten years numbers have been steadily increasing, and now figures reach a heady eight hundred thousand during the summer months with perhaps fifty thousand on the beaches on any one long, hot day. The end of a summer weekend sees winding snakes of cars all the way to the conurbations of Nîmes, Avignon and Marseilles.

But tourism *per se* was never encouraged in the Camargue; in fact it seems to have developed in spite of the Camargue. The delta is still infested with mosquitoes, and has dry, baking summers with the likelihood of the irritating and forceful *mistral* blowing a holiday to ruins. But the charisma of the white horses has given the area a glamour that reaches to Paris and competes with the Côte d'Azur for a northerner's dream holiday. Ranches have been transformed into hotels, offering riding holidays under a Camargue roof with all the romanticism of the *gardians'* life-style, with horse and bull games thrown in. There is always strong competition and some hostility between the Camargue's *cavaliers* and the outside horse-riders. Most visitors expect to be able to jump on a horse and ride off into the blue, but, because the horses are wild, and because the land is private property, no *gardian* is going to give a visitor that freedom.

Miraculously, the delta remains relatively unspoiled. There are only a couple of restaurants, and one or two garages: you can easily get stranded there and most visitors, if they are not camping, stay outside the Camargue. Two of the biggest ranches, the Mas de Cacharel and Mas Méjanes, have been transformed into big, thriving holiday centres (Méjanes even has a little train to show you the countryside). The quiet fishing village of Les-Saintes-Maries is now all white and looks like St Tropez, with boutiques selling riding clothes and bikinis, and with *crêpe* stands and discotheques. *Gardians'* huts have been built for holiday villas, hotels sprout along the roads that lead into Les-Saintes, and worst of all, a new village of holiday villas, with fake reed roofs and Provençal tiling, has been built a few kilometres outside Les-Saintes. This kind of development has shocked Camarguais. It was not wanted, nor intended; but slipped through the net of their new regulations as the power of real-estate defeated the rather weak laws.

In 1970, before matters got completely out of hand, however, the Camarguais converted the visions of Mistral and Baroncelli-Javon into fact and organised themselves into a Regional Park to protect two rather incompatible interests: their own and the territory's. They were driven to doing it, mainly because they began to see the imminent dangers from tourism and over-development. They knew their area had much of the past that they wanted to keep. The problem was how to lead it into the future while retaining that heritage.

It was not only tourists who upset them. Bird-watchers have their ruthless side too. They want to see as many birds as possible and to take home the best photographs. So, people who at home are law-abiding citizens are found wading out to the Flamingoes' colony, little thinking that their presence could frighten the adults off the nests and away, maybe, for ever. The Flamingoes' guard on the Étang de Fangassier tells the story of the German with his Haselblad cameras, who was spotted paddling out to the colony on a lilo and was heard to scream as he went under, "My Haselblads, my Haselblads". He was saved by the guard and ticked off for disturbing the Flamingoes, but he still cried for his Haselblads. Camarguais like that story.

Other visitors often regard the "private property" notices as an open invitation to wander—but then no one expects the ground to be quite so private or nature to be quite so in-hospitable. Just to get close enough to snap that bull, or that Egret fishing in the *roubine*! The Camargue has a stretch of beach that is wide and free and tolerates campers, and they pitch tents and happily dump cans and Coke bottles among the dunes, just off the Digue de la Mar and right into the Réserve lands. The coastline of the Camargue is already spoiled by this indiscriminate camping. There is no tide in the Mediterranean to clean up the beaches and no ugly scars are glossed over and washed out to sea. No toilets are provided for free campers, and nor are rubbish bins or removal services—for no one is paying. So the beach is dirty. The town of Les-Saintes is now constructing a camp site for several thousands, and is hoping to curb the free camping. But what will they do when the masses converge on the beach on a hot Sunday?

Similarly, ranchers can see that empty *gardian* huts have been sold to outsiders, looking for holiday homes. Their private *ferrades*, paid for by members of Clubs Taurins, have been invaded by hordes of eager voyeurs, wanting to see what these funny traditionalists are up to: and *manadiers* have felt they are becoming public property as people knock on their doors to ask to be shown what the *real* Camargue is like.

Somehow something had to stop the tide and the land had to be brought under the locals' control again. Just as piracy of property was a problem in the Middle Ages, so piracy of privacy has become a modern problem.

## Chapter 16

## A PARK FOR THE PEOPLE

THE CAMARGUE IS now presented as a prize example of
France's new regional nature parks, a *parc naturel régional*;
the scheme conceived during the rule of de Gaulle and first
instituted in 1967 with the coastline of Brittany. Brittany had
to be protected in some way from the further ravages of tourism
without also cutting off the lifeline of its indigenous population—
tourism. This kind of thinking was all part of the changing
face of nature conservation: that somehow a relationship has to
be worked out between the ever increasing industrial populations, more and more in need of leisure and relaxation, and the
vulnerability of the regions which could provide it.

The concept of national parks came from America in the late
nineteenth century. In those days, the American West offered
the far-seeing naturalist every opportunity for zoning off areas
of protection, with vast stretches of uncolonised land. In
Europe, things were never so easy, though ancient buildings
and traditions did act as a natural brake on the exploitation of
many pieces of land. The idea of the national parks was that they
should be very restrictive. They are usually made up of a
central zone of land, which is completely out of bounds to mass
tourism, and a peripheral belt where restrictions are not so
severe; tourist centres, hotels and shops are built and hunting
is permitted, though carefully controlled. Mostly, it was the
other developing countries, also largely unpopulated and which
could lay claim to virgin territory, that followed America's
pattern. In Europe, the non-Catholic countries followed first.
England, for example, formed the National Trust in 1895,

though in that she was behind the Swiss and the Swedes. Each country, however, interprets the law on whether to allow tourism or not in its own way.

In France, the problem of finding areas suitable for the requirements of national parks is obvious—what about the people already there who are dependent on the area for their livelihood? National parks are, therefore, found at the tops of mountain ranges, where the area can be zoned off and easily ringed by tourist facilities which provide compensation for the loss of revenue from the protected land. So the idea of the *parcs naturels régionaux* was arrived at. Their function, and the Camargue is the prime example of this, was to protect not only nature, but the livelihood of the residents, and to be able to offer some genuine diversion and relaxation for city dwellers.

The Camargue is still unique in that it already has the Réserve, a region of total control, at its centre, but the idea was to go beyond this and to organise the whole delta so that tourists could see wild black bulls, white horses and pink Flamingoes; could visit the feeding grounds of cattle and breeding grounds of aquatic species, without trampling everything underfoot on their way, and at the same time could acquire some information about what they were seeing. This does not mean that the Camargue is now a State controlled and financed nature paradise—far from it. In fact the scheme was very ambitious and optimistic, for in real terms the regional park meant that residents and property owners were able to keep some control of their own area and were able to oppose the delta turning into a national park.

One of the main differences between a national and a regional park is that the former is State financed and controlled and the latter is financed by the local community after the first three years. The other main difference is that in a national park hunting is necessarily forbidden, in a regional park it is not. The powerful hunting lobby among the Camargue proprietors was not going to let that slip away from them. So the compromise was made. It seemed a suitable formula, for the park was not State financed nor was it State controlled; and for a region with such a separatist streak as the Camargue, it seemed the right prescription. But, the ensuing lack of real power, or real finance, has proved to be its stumbling block.

The Park was created and its constitution drawn up in 1970, though it only began to function officially early in 1973 with a small team of officials operating from a rather dour house on the road leading to the Camargue from Arles. Its titular head is the linch-pin for the wide variety of local interests represented there: agriculturalists, stockbreeders, shops and restaurant keepers, hunters, fishermen, hotel keepers, nature conservationists and scientific researchers.

Its main problem will be lack of money. The Park will receive State help for its first three years, after which it has to find its own money. At the same time, it is committed to expensive projects, such as controlling tourism, and setting up reception centres and information kiosks. What its critics want to know is how can it uphold its ideological view as nature protector when that kind of involvement produces no income? Will it stick to its original plans or start subtly to develop tourism to bring in money? Regional power may sound fine, and it is admirable that there is a chance for local representatives to argue on behalf of their colleagues, but it would not do, surely, for the director of the Park to be seen pedalling up to the door of the wealthy landowner to suggest he take such and such a measure to the detriment of his agriculture, and to the advantage of the flora and fauna. These problems were made all too evident when the young and enthusiastic director resigned after the first eighteen months and went to seek peace and calm in Morocco.

Nevertheless, while at the beginning one of the problems was the conflicting interests of proprietors and farmers against those of the conservationists, the majority of landowners are now in favour of the Park and love to tell of their involvement in it. For it was the enthusiasm of many of the local proprietors that first led to there being any kind of park. The *Comité des soutiens*, a society of friends, and the *Comité des Propriétaires Camarguais*, were the prime movers.

At the beginning the farmers feared that they would be told what to grow and that this would make their living yet more precarious. Similarly, the shopkeepers of Les-Saintes-Maries felt that as the Park was against the growth of tourism it was trying to curtail their business. The Park actually has no power to make a farmer grow anything, but it is there to advise on the best use of the land. Most farmers now see the sense in discussing their crops with a view to an overall plan of the area. Education of the local people about why the Camargue is in danger, has been one of the important factors in bringing about the co-operation of some of the locals. It is the conservationists whose fears are most well-founded; they hope to see tourism not so much restricted as re-emphasised; people passing through the Camargue on their way to the beach should be made aware that they are passing through a nature reserve.

All the Park can hope to do is to try to control the harmful effects of tourism. Apart from attempting to clean up the camping situation, their plans centre on the idea of creating reception centres where information and guides would be available, where nature trails would be mapped out and people discouraged from wandering off the prescribed paths. There is talk of providing a large car park, thus refusing people permission to drive hell-bent down the narrow, exhausted roads. But such ideas bring to mind questions about freedom and the feared banality of the holiday village concept, where tourists are herded around like sheep.

The Park's main aims are really to deal with the larger problems. It has been laid down, for instance, that there is to be no new autoroute streaking its way across the Camargue, eating up the marshes so that people can get from Marseilles to Narbonne that much more quickly. The Camargue is still almost an island, and the Park has stated that there is to be no further bridging of the Rhône, which would ease transport and communications. Land use was the next sore point, and the Park has re-zoned the land available, designating agricultural areas, grazing land, *sansouire*, and building areas. Its biggest step was to lay down the stricture that for every new building there has to be a hundred and twenty-five acres (fifty hectares) of land, and the building can only be in an existing hamlet. This way they hope to be rid, once and for all, of the blight affecting other regions of France such as the Dordogne, or Languedoc-Roussillon, which have become playgrounds of the holiday-maker whether from home or abroad. Unfortunately, the once tiny commune, Pioch-Badet, slipped their net and the most obvious signs of the Park's amateurism were made plainly visible in the conglomeration of holiday villas that sprang up. Apart from those, there are scarcely any bijou residences to buy or let.

Even in its short history, things have not run totally smoothly for the Park. There have been fierce fights over some of the plans, as over, for instance, the proposed creation of a museum of the Camargue. For three months, the proprietors in the vicinity tried to defeat it fearing that it would attract souvenir hunters. But the museum was an exciting vision, being dedicated to re-creating the history of the Camargue and organised in connection with UNESCO. Finally, the proprietors stepped down, on the assurance that the museum would be non-profit making. But, in the meantime, small groups of the most powerful proprietors continue to plan how they can close off their land completely to tourists. Others, interested in educating the visitors, bend over backwards to help—putting on *ferrades* to be staged under the aegis of the Park and showing their traditional *modus vivendi* to schoolchildren wearing white cowboy hats, from Alsace. Not altogether a happy solution, as the staged *ferrade* lacks life, spontaneity, dynamism and fun. Still, what the Camarguais is saying, or trying to say, is that they are not going to witness the degradation of their precious way of life just because they are living in a glass house.

While the Camarguais may want to stand their ground with all the fierce pride of a separatist state, there is still the nagging doubt that, in these days, an anachronistic style of living is likely to be on a rather short lease. The Camarguais, involved in the traditional life style of bull and horse games, may detect a growing suspicion that he is becoming rather similar to the Indian on a Reserve, acting out a well-tried part for the sake of the Park's future. For the one or two *manadiers* who will actively help the Park in laying out their culture for the masses, the remainder may stay obdurately outside any control. And, as there is no State aid, the day may come when *manadiers* as a profession will die out. One of the most depressing prognostications for the future of the Camargue is that the day might come again when the area will be reduced to the state in which Baroncelli-Javon found it before the First World War. The Park should be able to prevent it—and the level of consciousness is definitely rising.

The one factor that may help ensure its survival is in the structure of the Park. The work of the Park is delegated to various commissions responsible for areas of activity; to decide on the reception centres, the style of tourist information, and educational material for agriculturalist and stock breeder; to watch over the hunter and shopkeeper; to keep an eye on town planning and land usage; to enforce the ban on hunting and fishing; to prevent the spoliation of the beaches and dykes; to ensure that electricity lines and telephone wires are placed underground; and to watch out for pollution in the water, air and soil.

The Camargue probably has as strong a chance of preserving its ancient traditions, and natural life, as any area in the world. The problems are not unique to the Rhône delta, but are felt by any area that is at once a nature reserve and a popular place for tourists. The question which, some time in the near future, will have to be answered is whether such areas should be preserved intact for the sake of the flora and fauna, or whether that would be a selfish attitude. Should the more beautiful areas be available for leisure and recreation? We all have equal rights to see and appreciate what is there. Conservationists feel that by educating visitors a new, responsible type of tourist will emerge. But is that really possible? I can only say to those who visit—tread softly.

# BIBLIOGRAPHY

Except for books on natural history which I have not included, texts and references about the Camargue are rare. I have indicated only those books that are specifically concerned with the Camargue; for wider reading on Provence there is a limitless supply. I have marked books I found only in the Bibliothèque Nationale in Arles thus *, and those in the British Museum thus †, for the more than casual reader.

Aldington, Richard, *Introduction to Mistral* (Heinemann, London, 1956).

Aubanel, Henri,* *Je Suis Manadier* (Paris, 1957).

Baranger, René,* *Un An de Gardianage en Camargue* (Avignon 1936).

Baranger, René,* *Camargue d'Aujourd'hui* (Paris, 1962).

Baroncelli-Javon, le Marquis Folco de,† *Babali* (Avignon, 1890).

Baroncelli-Javon, le Marquis Folco de,† *Blad de Luno* (Avignon, 1909).

Baroncelli-Javon, le Marquis Folco de,* *L'Élevage en Camargue de Taureaux* (Drome, 1931).

Benoit, Fernand,† *La Provence et Le Comtat Venaissin* (Paris, 1949).

Benoit, Fernand,† *La Camargue* (Paris, 1933).

Béthemont, Jacques,† *Le Riz et Le Mis en Valeur de la Camargue* (Revue de Géographie de Lyons, 1962).

Bicheron, Lucien, *Camargue Tourine* (Paris, 1974).

Bosco, Henri, *Malicroix* (Paris, 1948).

Campbell, Roy, *Collected Poems* (Faber, London, 1949).

Chapman, F. M., *Camps and Cruises of an Ornithologist* (London, 1908).

Charles-Roux, Jules,* *Livre d'Or de la Camargue* (Paris, 1916).

Clébert, Jean-Paul, *Provence Antique*, Volumes I and II (Paris, 1966, 1970).

Clébert, Jean-Paul, *Rêver de la Camargue* (Paris, 1956).

Clébert, Jean-Paul, *Gypsies*. Translated by Charles Duff (Penguin, London, 1963).

D'Arbaud, Joseph, *La Bête du Vaccarès* (Paris, 1926).

D'Arbaud, Joseph, *La Sauvagine* (Paris, 1929).

Daudet, Alphonse,† *Letters from My Windmill*. Translated by Edward Harris (Edinburgh, 1915).

Denizet, F.,* *La Camargue: Son Passé, Son Avenir* (Marseilles, 1931).

Des Vallières, Jean,† *Le Chevalier de la Camargue* (Paris, 1956).

Dorval, Yan, *La Nature et ses Merveilles: Les Parcs Naturels Français* (Paris, 1974).

Droit, Michel, *La Camargue* (Allen & Unwin, London, 1961).

Drouet, D. G., *Le Cheval Camargue* (France, 1910).

Dumas, Alexandre,† *Pictures of Travel in the South of France* (National Illustrated Library, London, 1851).

Durrell, Lawrence, *Spirit of Place* (Faber, London, 1969).

Edwards, Tudor, *The Lion of Arles: A Portrait of Mistral and his Circle* (Fordham University Press, New York, 1964).

Gadiot, Gerard,* *En Camargue: Taureaux, Chevaux et Gardians* (Paris, 1968).

Gallett, Étienne, *Les Flamants Roses de Camargue* (Paris, 1947).

Godefroy, Étienne Noel,* *Provence Historique*, Volume III (1953).

Hoffmann, Luc, *An Ecological Sketch of the Camargue*. In *British Birds*, Volume LI, pp. 321–49, September 1958.

Hoffmann, Luc, and Blondel, Jacques, *L'Originalité et le Rôle de la Réserve de Camargue*. (Bulletin des Réserves Naturelles et Ornithologiques de Belgique).

John, Augustus, *Chiaroscuro* (London, 1952).

Johnson, Alan, *Camargue Flamingoes* (International Flamingo Symposium, Slimbridge, July 1973).

Krippner, Monica, *Discovering the Camargue* (Hutchinson, London, 1960).

Mazel, A.,* *Notes sur la Camargue et Les-Saintes-Maries-de-la-Mer* (France, 1935).

Mauron, Marie, *La Camargue des Camarguais* (Paris, 1972).

Mistral, Frédéric, *Mes Origines*. English translation by Constance Maud (Edward Arnold, London, 1907).

Mistral, Frédéric, *Mireille*. English translation by C. H. Grant (Avignon, 1867).

Montherlant, Henri de, *The Matadors* (London, 1957).

Moyal, Maurice, *On the Road to Pastures New* (Phoenix House, London, 1956).

Oldham, R. D., *Earth Movements in the Rhône Delta* (*Nature*: April, 1930).

Parsons, Christopher, *A Bull called Marius* (BBC Publications, London, 1970).

Proal, Jeanne et Daunant, D. C., *Camargue* (Switzerland, 1955).

Quiqueran de Beaujeu,* *Provence Louée* (Arles, 1551).

Salem, Marcel,* *À la Gloire de la "Bouvino"* (Uzes, 1965).

Stendhal, *Memoires d'un Touriste* (Paris, 1838). Quoted in Jules Charles-Roux: *Livre d'Or de la Camargue* (Paris, 1916).

Varille, Mathieu,* *Trois de Camargue: D'Arbaud, Baroncelli-Javon et Hermann Paul* (Lyons, 1954).

Weber, Karl and Hoffmann, Luc, *Camargue: The Soul of a Wilderness* (Harrap, London, 1968).

Weber, Karl, *Camargue: un Pays Sauvage en Péril* (Switzerland, 1972).

Yeates, G. K., *Bird Life in Two Deltas* (Faber, London, 1946).

Yeates, G. K., *Flamingo City* (Country Life, London, 1950).

# INDEX and GLOSSARY

## By Michael Gordon

(Since many items appear *passim*, page numbers are given only for significant references.)

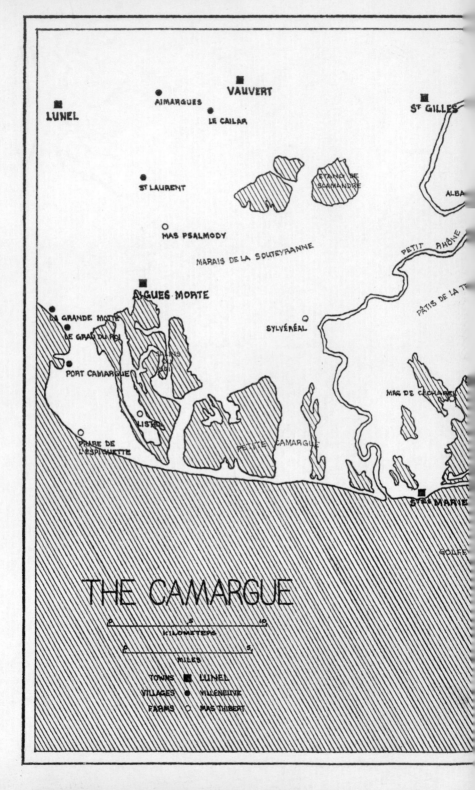

THE CAMARGUE

VAUVERT
LUNEL
AIMARGUES
LE CAILAR
St GILLES

St LAURENT
ÉTANG DE SCAMANDRE
ALBA

MAS PSALMODY

MARAIS DE LA SOUTEYRANNE
PETIT RHÔNE

AIGUES MORTE
PÂTIS DE LA TE

LA GRANDE MOTTE
LE GRAU DU ROI
SYLVÉRÉAL

PORT CAMARGUE
SALINS DU MIDI
MAS DE CACHAREL

LISTEL

PRABE DE L'ESPIGUETTE
PETITE CAMARGUE

Ste MARIE

GOLFE

0        5        10
KILOMETERS

0              5
MILES

TOWNS  ■ LUNEL
VILLAGES  ● VILLENEUVE
FARMS  ○ MAS THIBERT